A CRY FOR JUSTICE

The Churches and Synagogues Speak

edited by
Robert McAfee Brown
and
Sydney Thomson Brown

Paulist Press  New York/Mahwah

Library of Congress Cataloging-in-Publication Data

A Cry for justice: the churches and synagogues speak/edited by Robert McAfee Brown and Sydney Thomson Brown.
    p. cm.
Includes index.
ISBN 0-8091-3075-0
   1. United States—Religion—1960–   2. Christianity and justice.
3. Justice (Jewish theology) I. Brown, Robert McAfee, 1920–
II. Brown, Sydney Thomson, 1922–
BL2525.C77 1989
261.8′5—dc20   89-33660
                                                      CIP

Published by Paulist Press
997 Macarthur Boulevard
Mahwah, New Jersey 07430

Printed and bound in the
United States of America

Contents

Notes on the Contributors

WALDEN BELLO joined the Institute for Food and Development Policy as its senior analyst in Pacific affairs after spending more than a decade in Washington, D.C., lobbying to cut off aid to the Marcos dictatorship. He has authored and co-authored several books and articles, including: *American Lake: The Nuclear Peril in the Pacific.*

DAVID BIALE is the Koret Associate Professor of Jewish History and Director of the Center for Jewish Studies at the Graduate Theological Union in Berkeley. He has authored *Gershom Scholem: Kabbalah and Counterhistory* and *Power and Powerlessness in Jewish History* as well as articles on the history of the Jewish family.

JOHN A. COLEMAN, S.J. is Professor of Religion and Society at the Jesuit School of Theology and the Graduate Theological Union. He has authored *An American Strategic Theology* and is sociology of religion editor for the international Catholic journal, *Concilium.*

LONI HANCOCK is Mayor of Berkeley, California. She has served on the Advisory Board of the Working Assets Socially Responsible Money Market Fund, and was Executive Director of the Shalan Foundation, which provides funding and technical assistance to organizations involved in economic policy development.

KAREN LEBACQZ is Professor of Christian Ethics at the Pacific School of Religion in Berkeley, California. She has authored several books, including: *Justice in an Unjust World: Foundations for a Christian Approach to Justice,* and has written and lectured widely on issues in bioethics, feminist ethics and social justice.

JULIA K. MATSUI-ESTRELLA is director for the Pacific and Asian Center for Theologies and Strategies (PACTS), an ecumenical agency located at the Graduate Theological Union. She has served as an economic planner for Community Economics, Inc., Oakland, California, and is a member of the New Fellowship in Berkeley.

KAREN PAGET is director of the California Policy Seminar at the University of California. She holds a doctorate in political science from the University of Colorado, and was elected twice to the Boulder City Council. Dr. Paget has directed the Youth Project, a public foundation which supported social change organizations, in Washington, D.C.

JAMES W. RYDER is the President of the International Longshoremen's and Warehousemen's Union (ILWU) Local 6 in Oakland, California, and serves on the ILWU International Executive Board. Trained as an anthropologist, Mr. Ryder has worked as a research specialist in demographics at the University of California, Berkeley.

J. ALFRED SMITH, SR. is the Senior Pastor of The Allen Temple Baptist Church in Oakland, California. He is former President of the Progressive National Baptist Convention, USA, and former Dean of the American Baptist Seminary of the West. Pastor Smith is an author and Adjunct Professor in Bay Area seminaries.

EDWARD VORIS developed *A Cry for Justice* while on the staff of The Center for Ethics and Social Policy, for their Ethics in Economic Life Program. An Episcopal layperson, he serves on the Economic Justice Commission of the Diocese of California and co-directs Ocean View Center, a neighborhood development in Berkeley.

JOAN WALSH is a writer and associate editor at Pacific News Service whose work has appeared in *Ms., Mother Jones, The Nation, In These Times,* and many local newspapers. She has served as a consultant on family policy and poverty issues to the Catholic Legislature.

JOHN OLIVER WILSON teaches at the University of California, Berkeley, in the School of Business Administration and the Graduate School of Public Policy. He is Chief Economist at the Bank of America and serves on several corporate Boards of Directors. Mr. Wilson has authored several books, including: *After Affluence: Economics to Meet Human Needs.*

Special thanks to
Ed Voris
without whom
it would never have happened

Preface

Robert N. Bellah

The papers assembled in *A Cry for Justice* provide an invaluable resource for continuing and deepening the discussion of economic justice which various religious groups have initiated. Ours is a pluralistic society—religiously, politically and culturally pluralistic. Consequently it is appropriate that the present volume is pluralistic. Not only are a variety of positions presented, but there are serious tensions and even conflicts between them. What we are presented with is not an easy consensus but a vital argument about the responsibility of religious people for economic justice.

The cry for justice comes from the poor and the oppressed and from those for whom the existence of the poor and the oppressed in a society, and potentially a world, of affluence is a scandal. All of the religious groups are concerned with the terrible poverty that afflicts so many in the world today and with what we can do to mitigate that poverty. Yet the biblical teaching about poverty is complex and not easily applied to the contemporary world. In both Testaments the poor are seen as especially close to God. Indeed "the poor" and "the pious" are virtually synonymous. Jesus said, "Blessed are the poor." Conversely the rich are depicted as far from God. Jesus said that it is easier for a camel to pass through the eye of a needle than for a rich man to enter the kingdom of heaven. Yet what we have here is not a biblical foreshadowing of class struggle. The poor are close to God because they depend on nothing but God. The rich are far from God because they worship their riches and falsely believe in their own self-sufficiency. Further, the poor are blessed because they share even the little they have—one meaning of the story of the loaves and the fishes—whereas the rich find it hard to share—the story

1

of the wealthy young ruler. We are called on to share what we have with the poor (Matthew 25), but the Bible does not advocate that we make the poor rich, for that would only alienate them from God.

Albert Borgmann has pointed out that the poverty in today's world seems very different from biblical poverty. We are faced with what he calls brutal poverty, the terrible, unnecessary poverty in a world economically and technologically capable of eliminating poverty. And we middle-class Americans live in the midst of what he calls advanced poverty, the spiritually debilitating affluence, related to the biblical depiction of the rich, that is in an important sense the cause of brutal poverty. Our secular politicians and activists concentrate on the elimination of brutal poverty, without concerning themselves very much with advanced poverty. There are two problems with this approach. One is that if it succeeded it would only promote those in a state of brutal poverty to a state of advanced poverty, decreasing physical suffering but increasing spiritual alienation, and not addressing the real problem of the sickness of our form of society. But the second, more serious, problem is that the secular politicians and activists are unlikely to succeed in eliminating brutal poverty if they do not address the problem of advanced poverty which is its cause.

If there is any validity in this argument, then some of the secular criticisms of religious communities contained in the later chapters of this book are misplaced. Both brutal poverty and advanced poverty are not just economic and political conditions; they are symptoms of spiritual sickness. To be sure they require us to think about economic and political changes, but at a deeper level what they require of us is conversion. Consequently those who criticize the religious bodies for being insufficiently political are only partly right. Their own faith in purely political solutions is surely misplaced, as we have learned over and over again when even radical political change is unaccompanied by spiritual transformation.

In a recent issue of the Young Lawyers Division *Affiliate* newsletter, Robert M. Hayes, general counsel for the National Coalition for the Homeless, observed:

All you have to do is show a lawyer the desperation of life on the streets and you have a convert. All you have to do is see homelessness, smell homelessness, feel homelessness, and you know it's wrong. One homeless child will move an attorney far faster and further than the most eloquent sermon anyone could give.

It is interesting that Hayes uses the word "convert," but perhaps the problem is deeper than he realizes. The culture of advanced poverty inoculates us against seeing, smelling or feeling homelessness. We may be sure that there are many lawyers (and other middle-class people) who do not, perhaps cannot, look at homelessness. Looking moves to conversion, but conversion must already be at work in order for a person to be able to look. The articles in this book and the statements by religious bodies on which they are based can contribute to the process of conversion which will enable us to look and to be transformed by the looking. Sydney and Robert Brown in their concluding chapter suggest that we need not only to look, but also to listen. We need to hear directly the cry for justice of the poor and the oppressed and to engage in discussion with them as to appropriate actions. I would certainly endorse such discussions wherever possible. Through such discussions, and with the help of the churches and synagogues, middle-class religious people need to begin to address our own advanced poverty, to open ourselves to a process of conversion that moves beyond "helping the poor" to changing our lives, not only individually but the social structures in which we live.

Perhaps not surprisingly the mainline Protestant statements remain closest to the agenda of secular reform. The problems they discern and the solutions they offer are worthy of serious discussion. They address many of the glaring problems in our current social arrangements. We can ask, however, whether they press far enough in their analysis of advanced poverty and whether they press us sharply enough toward openness to conversion. As Karen Lebacqz points out, the Church of the Brethren, with its emphasis on a radical life of discipleship, provides a valuable emphasis from which mainline Protestants could well learn.

John Wilson's contrast of the Protestant and Catholic statements is also suggestive. He argues that the Protestant statements largely accept existing institutional arrangements but argue for changing priorities between them, advocating increased government intervention and a narrowing of corporate autonomy, but not essentially questioning the nature of government or corporations. The Catholic bishops on the other hand, he argues, challenge the whole existing structure of economic arrangements in the United States and argue for a more participational institutional life at all levels. We might translate this to mean that the Catholics are more concerned with institutional conversion than the Protestants are, probably because they were not nearly as involved as Protestants in the creation of our current institutions. Yet even in the Catholic letter *Economic Justice for All,* there is an ambiguity. At moments the bishops seem to be arguing that solving the economic problems of the poor is the basic issue. At other moments they question the whole structure of a society devoted to private acquisition and individual autonomy, insisting that the dignity of the individual person is only realized in and through community. It is the latter concern that recognizes the need for a radical conversion beyond all economic and political programs.

If the basic problem in the contemporary world is simply to turn the have-nots into haves, then the political and economic struggle is central and the religious bodies have a significant but minor role to play. They can usefully be encouraged by secular activists to play that role more vigorously. But if our problems have to do with the whole notion that having is the meaning of life, then the role of the religious bodies may be more decisive. Indeed if an exclusive concern for having is moving us toward global economic and ecological disaster, then biblical poverty may not be an alternative suitable only for small dedicated groups like the Catholic Workers. Biblical poverty, the notion that we must let go of everything we have and depend only on God and our neighbor, may be the only thing that will save us. In that case, along with our political and economic concerns, we should also pray for the grace that is the only possible basis for the conversion of ourselves and our institutions.

PART I

THE SITUATION

1. Responding to "A Cry for Justice": Overall Reflections Plus a Few Nuts and Bolts

Robert McAfee Brown

Then the Lord said [to Moses], "I have seen the affliction of my people who are in Egypt, and I have heard their cry because of their taskmasters; I know their suffering, and *I have come down to deliver them* out of the hand of the Egyptians . . .

"And now, behold, the cry of the people of Israel has come to me, and I have seen the oppression with which the Egyptians oppress them. Come, *I will send you to Pharaoh that you may bring forth my people.*"

Exodus 2:7–8, 10

Moses is in a tough spot. He has had to flee to Midian in order to escape from the long arm of the Egyptian law, galvanized by well-founded rumors that he had murdered an Egyptian guard. An "All Points Alert" has been circulated, offering a handsome reward to the person who tips off the authorities as to Moses' whereabouts.

God does not seem to be taking Moses' personal plight very seriously. There are larger matters on the divine horizon, namely the plight of the entire people of Israel, and God is suggesting that Moses must re-enter Egypt and deal directly with the oppression and injustice that are plaguing his people. That this will cause Moses some personal inconvenience is not to be allowed to deter him from responding to the call.

As the above quotations make clear, there are two parts to the message Moses receives. Although they seem initially to be contradictory, they are finally complementary, and they have everything to do with the subject matter of this book.

The *first,* and reassuring, word is that God has heard "the cry of the people"—a cry for justice in a situation of injustice—and has promised to "come down and deliver them." Whatever trouble we moderns may have with some of the imagery of the passage—a deity on a kind of celestial escalator between heaven and earth, apparently reversible at the whim of the divine will, not to mention a context in which the voice of God is coming from a bush that is burning but not burning up—the bedrock assurances of which the passage speaks outstrip the imagery with which they are surrounded: God is a God who is not aloof from the plight of people suffering injustice and oppression; a God, in other words, who not only hears their cry, but as a consequence actively intervenes on their behalf. The unjust situation will be redressed, the cry will not have gone for naught, God's righteousness will be maintained, and the people's plight will be overcome. Quite an agenda, even for God.

The *second,* and demanding, word, however, is a reminder that the promise of God's involvement in establishing justice on earth is predicated on human involvement as well. There is no possibility of sitting back and watching the Almighty move into high gear. For in addition to the promise of divine help, Moses is told that he (along with the rest of the Israelites) is to be the short-range means by which the long-range plans of God are fulfilled. The message is unequivocal: "I will send *you* to Pharaoh that *you* may bring forth my people."

This is a different matter altogether, and Moses tries to duck the assignment, pointing out, rather lamely, that he st-t-t-utters (a malady no doubt enhanced in its intensity by his realization that the old murder rap may surface again), but he is not to be given the privilege of remaining on the sidelines. So at the divine behest he returns to Egypt, enters into the maelstrom of court intrigue and power politics, from which he and the children of Israel emerge (thanks as well to some spectacular assistance from the Almighty) with the shackles of economic and political oppression at least temporarily removed, and new possibilities for creative living staring them in the face.

An Old Story Becomes Contemporary

The ancient story (like most ancient stories emanating from the same source) turns out to coincide rather nicely with our own story. We discover that we are descendants of the actors in the ancient drama, whether we are Jews or Christians, and we face the same kinds of choices today that faced the folks back then.

The faith we inherit assures us, for example, that whenever there is a fresh "cry of the people"—a contemporary cry for justice—God is no more indifferent to such a cry now than God was then. God wants justice, and the world in which God has placed us is a world in which it is clear that there could be justice for *all,* but in which it is equally clear that there is justice only for a *few.* And a situation in which there is justice only for a few is by definition a situation of injustice. The first word for us today, then, is that God proposes to do something about this parlous state of affairs.

And it is in the light of that conviction that the second word to Moses becomes a second word for us as well, i.e. that the God who hears the "cry for justice" elects to use us now, just as Moses was used then, to work for justice. We are called to go to the modern equivalents of Pharaoh's court, not only to intercede for victims, but to empower victims to go there and plead and act on their own behalf. Whether Pharaoh's many courts today will listen to this "cry," or ignore it, or deflect it, or withstand it, or be brought down by it, remains to be seen.

The religious bodies of our nation today—Catholic, Protestant, Jewish—have tried, with varying degrees of success, to position themselves within this ancient drama turned contemporary. They have tried to be faithful to both parts of the Moses story: (a) that God cares about justice and works to bring it into being, and (b) that all who worship this God are likewise called to care about justice and work to bring it into being. The documents that are subjected to scrutiny in this volume are a sampling of specific and practical attempts by a variety of religious groups to speak about their corporate responsibility for involving all religiously-minded people in the never-ending struggle for justice.

Loud Query: Is Such Activity Appropriate?

Their commitment to doing this, however, is not happily received by everyone. In some quarters (perhaps one should say "in *many* quarters"), there is strong resistance to churches and synagogues taking on what seem, to the critics, to be tasks and concerns that go beyond the scope (let alone the competence) of such groups.

This mood is sufficiently widespread that we must hear a rundown of the complaints if we are to continue to take the concerns of the present volume seriously. From many points of view, then, and with varying degrees of stridency, we hear such charges as the following:

1. For the churches and synagogues to speak about "secular" matters such as economics is to neglect their real task, which is to acquaint us with the things of the spirit.

The unstated theological premise behind this argument is that there is a gigantic split between the "sacred" and the "secular" which religious bodies must honor. It is a considerable irony that both Judaism and Christianity are centrally dedicated to the proposition that such a split is illegitimate. In Judaism, God is the creator of the world and in God's eyes the world is good. God furthermore seeks to work out the divine purposes here on earth (witness the Moses story); the Hebrew scriptures refer to "earth" five times as often as to "heaven." It is the central tenet of Christianity that this same God, "the God of Abraham, Isaac and Jacob," and the God of Sarah, Leah and Rachel, was "made flesh" (a particularly offensive notion in the Greek culture in which it was first proclaimed) and indwelt a fully human life. In both traditions one cannot speak of God without speaking of the world, nor speak of the world without speaking of God. They are inseparable.

Why, then, the persistence of the claim that churches and synagogues are straying from their task when they reflect on the ordering (or disordering) of life on earth? The real objection seems not to be that religious bodies speak of "worldly things," but that in doing so they tend to challenge the present arrangement of worldly things. As long as "the way things are" receives the blessing of church and synagogue, there is no problem. The objection, in other words, is not so much that religious bodies speak about economics, but that they tend to speak critically about U.S. economics, and that cuts too close to the bone. The complaint is at least as old as Isaiah, who reports that he was enjoined by the right-wing critics of his day to "speak to us smooth things" (Is 30:18). Isaiah refused. So, at their best, do the churches and synagogues.

2. *Religious leaders are not experts on matters of economics and they should therefore remain silent, or confine their observations to matters on which they have expertise, such as prayer, sacraments, or life after death.*

It is true that ordination does not endow its recipients with unique economic wisdom, but it is also true that statements on economics by churches and synagogues are the product of the involvement of experts in such matters, as well as members of the clergy or rabbinate. The Catholic bishops, for example, went to special lengths to make sure that hundreds of lay experts had input at every stage in the creation of their document on the economy, and other groups have employed similar safeguards to make sure they were not speaking out of ignorance.

In addition, along with much specificity, there is an admirable restraint in the documents about claiming too much for their conclusions. All recognize that the shift from theological premises to economic conclusions is tricky if not treacherous ground, and rather than try to provide full-blown economic systems, the statements are intended to provide materials for reflection out of which individuals and groups who read them can be stimulated to further reflection, and action, of their own.

3. *The production of "controversial" documents threatens to divide religious bodies, and should therefore be avoided for the sake of unity.*

The claim ignores the fact that "unity" can sometimes be bought at too heavy a price, namely blandness at best and disregard of truth at worst. It also presupposes that controversy is an evil thing and that static uniformity is preferable to healthy diversity.

But the most serious shortcoming of the argument is its assumption that there is some desirable "neutral" position that is preferable to taking sides. But on issues of life and death (which matters of economic structures certainly are) the attempt to be neutral is both impossible and immoral. As Desmond Tutu, Anglican archbishop of South Africa, has said, "If you are neutral in a situation of injustice, you have chosen the side of the oppressor. If an elephant has his foot on the tail of a mouse, and you say you are neutral, the mouse will not appreciate your neutrality." The attempt to be "neutral," in other words, means putting the not inconsiderable weight of the religious bodies on the side of the status quo, and human beings as well as mice might have a few instructive comments for us about how "neutral" that really is.

4. *If religious bodies are going to speak about economic questions, they should first put their own houses in order before presuming to lecture the rest of us.*

On one level, the comment is intended to have a paralyzing effect: What Christian or Jewish organization can ever become pure enough to be entitled to criticize the internal structure of other social groups?

But on another level, the remark is quite appropriate, and it is instructive to note that a number of the documents make this very point themselves: as participants in the economic life of the society they must be held to at least as exacting standards of social justice within their own lives as other groups. Indeed, they would accept the notion that they can only expect to be taken seriously to the degree that they are seeking to embody themselves what they are proposing for others.

The reasons why religious bodies *should* speak out on matters of injustice in the world are contained by implication in the rebuttals to the four points above. Reduced to its simplest terms, the argument insists that both Judaism and Christianity explicitly repudiate the dualistic assumption that the religious gaze should be focused exclusively on a world other than this one, and both likewise affirm the contrary assumption that *this world* is the scene of divine activity. This means that at whatever point the divine intention for God's creatures is being frustrated or openly opposed, it is the *duty* of all religious bodies—and individuals—to challenge and seek to change that situation. Few things have as much impact on the possibility for fulfilled human lives as whether or not people have enough to eat, drink, and wear—whether they have adequate shelter, a chance for medical care, and so on. So rather than being optional subject matter for Jewish and Christian reflection, such issues must always be found at the *center* of discussion and action. And this is precisely what the documents under consideration in the present volume are trying to achieve.

The Documents Themselves

Juan Luis Segundo, a Uruguayan Jesuit, has said that the starting point of liberation theology is not a theological claim, or even an exclusively "religious" insight, but one that can be shared by all people, whether Christians, Jews, or secularists. Those who do not resonate to the claim, he says, will never understand what liberation theology is all about. The claim is clear and unadorned: "The world should not be the way it is."

The phrase is invoked here not to initiate a discussion of liberation theology, but to suggest that it represents an appropriate, even mandatory, approach for all those concerned about human justice in the world today. If all were well in the world today there would be no need for pronouncements by churches and synagogues, and we could all attend more usefully to other concerns. But if there is anything upon which the variegated documents assessed in this volume agree, it is on the legitimacy of Fr. Segundo's starting point. The documents may, to be sure, disagree on the specifics of how to change the world in order to make it better, and they frequently do, but they form a coherent unity in their implicit, and often explicit, acceptance of this shared presupposition.

The documents, considered in varying degrees of detail below, come from the following religious groups: the United States Catholic Conference, the Canadian Conference of Catholic Bishops, the Unitarian Universalist Association, the National Jewish Community Relations Advisory Council, the Union of American Hebrew Congregations, the National Council of Churches of Christ in the U.S.A., the American Baptist churches, the Society of Friends (Quakers), the Church of the Brethren (Mennonites), the Christian Church (Disciples of Christ), the Episcopal Church in the U.S.A., the Lutheran Church in America, the United Presbyterian Church, U.S.A., the United Church of Christ, the United Church of Canada, and the United Methodist Church.

The list is arbitrary in the sense that many similar groups could have been included and are not, but it is representative in the sense that a wide enough variety of religious traditions is represented so as to indicate both points of similarity and difference, in style, content, and recommendations.

What is the status of the documents produced by these groups? What weight do they carry within their own tradition, and what import can they have for us? The answer is complex. None of them claim, "You *have* to believe this to be a good (Methodist, Catholic, Quaker, Jew)." By the same token, however, they imply, "If you *are* a good (Methodist, Catholic, Quaker, Jew), you need to listen carefully to what is being said here, since it represents a responsible attempt to articulate the tradition in which you stand." Most of the documents, in this ecumenical era, are also saying something more: "Although this particular document is the work of (Methodists, Catholics, Quakers, Jews), it does not speak exclusively to that tradition but to the whole body of concerned human beings, whether 'religious' or not, who think that struggling with these issues is worthwhile and necessary." The greatest authority surely inheres in the statements of the Catholic bishops, since bishops are viewed in that tradition as arbiters of the teaching authority of the church. But even there, opposition to the bishops' letter on economics was engendered by certain lay groups within Catholicism who felt it was too "leftist." The formula used by the World Council of Churches, when it votes on similar matters of social concern at a world assembly, is probably the best rule-of-thumb for assessing the weight of similar documents on their constituencies. After voting, a World Council assembly "commends the document to the churches for appropriate study and action," leaving it to the member churches to decide what, from their perspective, is "appropriate."

The Structure of This Book

In the best of all possible worlds, all the documents in their entirety would be available, and it is the hope of the contributors to this volume that a companion volume fitting this need may shortly appear. Lacking that, a special effort has been made in Part II (after an important initial essay in Part I on "Setting the Stage") to give sufficiently detailed accounts of the documents on social justice of the three major religious traditions in the United States, so that readers will have enough data to begin to make their own appraisals of what has been reviewed. (Information about securing any or all of the documents is contained in the Appendix.)

As an aid to this evaluative adventure, Part III presents several distinctly—and deliberately—different assessments of the documents, from the point of view of corporations, labor unions, and the poor of the third world. One of the contributors early on expressed a fear that the book would lack focus, since it would represent such a variety of points of view. The potential defect, however, must be claimed as a virtue: the point of the book is not only to impart information, but to confront readers with differing interpretations so that they will have the resources out of which not only to form views of their own, but to begin to act upon them.

It is the latter point that informs Part IV. Recognizing that the fate of most religious pronouncements, however able, is to collect dust in the archives, suggestions are made, from a variety of perspectives, for implementing the statements' concerns in the political and ecclesiastical arenas. The specificity of these chapters should give readers sufficient "handles" to begin their own active engagement with the issues.

The project was initiated by the Center for Ethics and Social

Policy of the Graduate Theological Union in Berkeley, California, by Ellen Teninty and Ed Voris. Authors were chosen not only because of professional expertise but also so that their geographical proximity would make possible the joint planning of the book. The various authors met twice as a group for extended sessions, once to work out specific topics and assignments together and set the overall direction of the book, and later to share presentations of their own prospective chapters, in order to garner suggestions from the other contributors and make sure there would not be needless overlapping. The volume is thus offered as a unitary whole, rather than as a haphazard collection of discrete essays. It should go without saying (but let the record be clear) that each writer is responsible only for the material in his or her chapter.

It is the conviction of the authors and editors that the documents under consideration are important statements, that they lay significant tasks on Christians, Jews, and "all persons of good will," and that it is worthwhile to become acquainted with them, reflect on them, and then make our own responses in the deeds that we do separately and together.

2. Setting the Scene

Joan Walsh

Anyone looking to capture the civic culture of the 1980s could hardly do better than a February 1988 feature spread on panhandling in the Washington *Post*. Reprinted in newspapers across the country, the two-article feature was an in-depth look at how individuals and society respond to poor people who ask them for money, written with the sociological seriousness reserved for truly national phenomena like day care arrangements, the crisis in public education, or how communities cope with AIDS.

"In every city, the moral question remains," the *Post* explained. "When confronted by the plaintive request, 'Got a quarter?', most pedestrians seem to have one of two reactions: They give money because they feel pressured, or they don't give money and they feel guilty. Either way, it's not a happy experience." A New York professional recounted the scene on her walk to work: "An average of four or five people actually will ask for money, and more have signs. . . . There's a little old lady who asks me for pennies to buy coffee, there's women with children, an older man who says 'God bless you' even when you don't give him anything, young men who curse. I've crossed the street to get away from people so I won't have to feel guilty. Some people take more cabs."

A reader from another era might think the article parody or farce. Someone from another culture might think it tragic, that panhandlers are such a common feature of the urban landscape that a major newspaper could catalogue the different ways individuals respond to them. But the feature spread was vivid proof of how the last decade's conservative political shift has succeeded

17

in privatizing what once were public responsibilities. In Ronald Reagan's America, more people came face to face with the moral and economic challenge of helping those who fell through the tattered safety net. Responsibility for tough judgments about the need, eligibility and worthiness of those who seek help—the kind of judgments once reserved for social service bureaucrats—trickled down to individual citizens in the late 1980s.

The religious communities found themselves in a comparable predicament at the decade's start, when the early victims of the shrinking of the public sector turned to religious-run charitable institutions for help. Increasingly, religious leaders realized that they were filling an ethical vacuum as well as an economic one. They saw that the disappearance of public resources for those in need was linked to a loss of publicly shared values, the lack of a common notion of public good. The statements described in this book represent an attempt to fill both vacuums.

The "New Poor"

Ronald Reagan's election represented a radical redirection in American public life. The economic, social and moral drift of the late 1970s created a ready audience for Reagan's evocation of a simpler, perhaps mythic era, when families took care of their own, businesses were trusted to watch out for employees, and churches ministered to the needy. That Reagan's election-eve challenge to voters—"Are you better off now than you were four years ago?"—had such a lasting resonance was a measure of American social insecurity.

Implicit in Reagan's election was a sense that security didn't lie in common efforts to address problems, but in the unfettering of individual rights and responsibilities. Returning tax dollars and questions of values to individual families and businesses was an effort to shrink the public sector, restore the power of the private sector, and establish self-interest as the measure of political utility and common sense in the United States.

In tune with the times, questions of morality in public life shifted to the religious sector, one of the few settings where urges for community and social cooperation could be satisfied. Indeed, belief in the power of public policy or active government, along with compassion for those left out of the new social and economic order, became a private, quasi-spiritual matter in the 1980s, comparable to belief in God. It's no wonder that today religious groups are leaders in articulating a new public philosophy.

But the religious communities were also galvanized toward economic and political activism by the boom in the number of people seeking their charitable help in the early 1980s. Christian and Jewish philanthropy has always provided a safety net in the U.S., where even in generous times provision was not made for public assistance to all who needed it. The post-depression welfare state had sought to help those who couldn't help themselves —the elderly, the disabled, and women and children left without male support. Unemployed, able-bodied men fell into the category of the "undeserving poor," and assisting them fell to charity—the religious-run rescue missions and soup kitchens, for instance, located in urban "Skid Rows."

But in the early 1980s religious groups began to see a "new poor," of women and children, newly unemployed men, even whole families using their services. In the cities, many were victims of the economic recession of the early decade; in rural areas, they were refugees from the farm crisis rocking American agriculture. Some were casualties of the welfare cutbacks initiated at the start of the Reagan administration. Religious-run charities like soup kitchens, food pantries and homeless shelters couldn't keep pace with the new demands for help.

"In San Francisco, the churches found more and more people literally on their doorsteps in the early 1980s," recalls Kathleen Connolly of the Food Box, a cooperative project of more than one hundred religious denominations in the city. With the Food Box, religious groups began to coordinate their food giveaway efforts. But the agency soon found itself doing more than food distribution. "We saw that a lot of people don't just need food—their rent is going unpaid, their kids are sick, they're eligible for welfare but aren't getting it," Connolly said. "So we work with a lot of social service agencies to get them whatever help they need." Eighty percent of those whom the Food Box serves are women and children.

By the end of 1983, religious groups were filling the social service gaps so notably that the Reagan administration's Task Force on Hunger could actually conclude that there was no hunger problem in America, thanks to the network of voluntary charitable agencies providing food assistance to those who needed it. But while many religious efforts across the country doubled and tripled their social service budgets throughout the decade, few could serve all who needed their help.

The prospect of becoming a permanent, institutional safety net daunted a growing number of religious leaders. Says Pat Theisen of the Washington, D.C.–based Interfaith Action for Economic Justice: "The churches really attempted to meet the need, and discovered they couldn't—that government had to do more."

Wrote the urban bishops of the Episcopal Church: "Our local congregations and dioceses are responding modestly well to the personal side of the economic crisis—with soup kitchens and overnight shelters and counseling programs. But is not the hour overdue for us to question more seriously and more publicly whether it really makes sense to sustain emergency 'Safety net' activities . . . without insisting that changes be made in those public policies and business practices which, however unintentionally, have served to create the poverty in the first place?" A broad array of religious denominations answered yes.

The Pervasiveness of Poverty

The most disturbing feature of modern American life that the religious economic justice statements seek to address is the persistent number of people living in poverty. After following a steady downward curve from the mid-1960s through the 1970s, poverty rates arched upward in the 1980s. There were 4.3 million more Americans who fell into poverty between 1979 and 1985 alone, and most of them were women and children. As the U.S. Catholic bishops note, "We are the first industrialized nation in the world in which children are the poorest age group." One out of four American children under the age of six lives below the poverty line today.

Cutbacks in welfare eligibility, which pushed 557,000 people off the public assistance rolls in the early 1980s, were one culprit in rising poverty rates. Reagan administration spending cuts hit programs for low-income Americans twice as hard as other social programs.

Yet increasingly in the 1980s, the "poor" are not just the clients of public welfare agencies, but workers supporting families on low-wage jobs. Between 1978 and 1986, the number of adults working at least thirty hours a week but still living in poverty jumped fifty-two percent, to include seven million Americans—more than a third of all poor adults in the U.S., and twice the number of adults receiving Aid to Families with Dependent Children, for instance. Others who make up the "new poor" have worked their whole lifetimes, only to be thrown out of work in plant closures, layoffs and slowdowns.

Significantly, the economic justice statements of the religious community don't isolate the poor, but place them on a continuum of national economic insecurity brought about by profound economic shifts, most notably the nation's transition from a manufacturing to a service and information economy. In its statement on *Christian Faith and Economic Life,* the United Church of Christ points to the 11.5 million industrial workers who lost their jobs between 1979 and 1984. Of five million surveyed in 1986, a third were still unemployed, and almost half of those with new jobs took substantial pay cuts.

The shift from a manufacturing to a service economy has changed the nature and expectations of employment in the U.S., perhaps permanently. Wrote the Catholic bishops: "By 1990, service industries are expected to employ seventy-two percent of the labor force. Much of the job growth in the 1980s is expected to be in traditionally low-paying, high-turnover jobs such as sales, clerical, janitorial and food service. Too often these jobs do not have career ladders leading to higher skilled, higher paying jobs. Thus, the changing industrial and occupational mix in the U.S. economy could result in a shift toward lower paying and lower skilled jobs."

The Expansion of Economic Insecurity

Manufacturing workers and the poor have not been the only casualties of the wage and workforce cuts employed by American business in the face of international competition. Record numbers of middle and upper income managers lost jobs in the scaledowns conducted by business in the 1970s and 1980s. And the explosion of business mergers and acquisitions has meant job loss not just for production employees, but for management personnel who are often made redundant when two businesses become one. Even unsuccessful takeovers trigger layoffs and paycuts because the "victim" is usually saddled with new debt incurred to fend off the attempt. In the San Francisco Bay area alone, half of the seventy largest publicly held corporations have experienced successful or attempted takeovers since 1984.

Many of these displaced managerial workers have been forced into the so-called "contingent" workforce of part-time, temporary, contract or seasonal employees, and "consultants" brought in by firms for short term projects. As much as a quarter of the workforce now labors in the contingent sector, and many are still doing the work they once did as salaried employees— data processors transferred from offices to home computer terminals, for instance, and public relations consultants laid off by large corporations. Such workers have no employer-paid health or retirement benefits, and, by definition, none of the job security once associated with steady employment.

Thus the landscape of economic insecurity that the religious community has surveyed includes large portions of the middle class. Four times as many people fell out of the middle class as rose above it in the last decade. Between 1968 and 1983, the middle "fifth" of Americans saw their share of national wealth decline to seventeen percent, while the richest fifth's share grew from 33.8 to 38 percent. Home ownership, to many the symbol of middle class status, became a more difficult achievement. In 1949 a median income wage-earner spent fourteen percent of his or her gross monthly income on mortgage payments; today their counterpart spends forty-four percent.

The Impact on the Family

While real family income may have risen, if unevenly, over the last two decades, a 1988 Congressional Budget Office report attributed that to most families' sending second earners, usually wives, into the labor market. Without fanfare, that has meant the end of the forty hour week—now most families rely on fifty to eighty hours of labor, albeit by two persons, to achieve the living standards they once maintained with one forty hour a week worker. That, in turn, has changed the nature of what it means to be middle class, and of middle class family life, permanently. Observing the changes in American family life at every income level, wrought at least partly by economic stress, the religious communities have made support for families central to their economic justice demands.

In two short decades the traditional American norm of a breadwinner-father and homemaker-mother went the way of the trolley car. Inflation and wage erosion made two earners a necessity for most families, evident in the dramatic jump in working mothers—from forty-five to sixty-two percent—just since 1977. In the same period, paradoxically, rising rates of divorce and unmarried parenthood have left many women with sole responsibility for their children, with the resulting high poverty rates for women and children noted above.

The transformation of the American family produced cultural shocks not yet fully absorbed. Unlike the rest of the industrialized world, no national "family policy" exists in the U.S. to mediate the growing conflicts between work and family. American parents have no guaranteed parental leave, child care assistance, flexible work hours or family allowances—supports that their western counterparts take for granted. One result is that children are growing up with less moral, emotional and material caretaking than previous generations. A child care experience is now the norm for American children, and yet the availability of reliable care is, in the pungent comment of one national expert, "a cosmic crap shoot." In the state of California, for instance, one million more children need child care than can be served by existing, licensed resources.

Again, religious institutions have tried to fill this caretaking breach. Jewish community centers and YMCAs and YWCAs have long run child care centers, for instance, often at subsidized rates, for working parents in their communities. But again, religious agencies came to realize that they were filling an institutional responsibility vacuum. The private sector has reduced the wage and benefit commitments to American families that it assumed during post-World War II prosperity. Families, forced to send a second earner into the workforce to survive financially, face a huge caretaking gap in the home, where women once labored unpaid. And in the 1980s, government has been told to do less, meaning that social programs have not emerged to fill the breach.

To close that responsibility gap, a large portion of the religious communities have advocated public and private sector support for families facing new economic demands. Concluded the Presbyterian Church in *Towards a Just, Caring and Dynamic Political Economy,* "The old-fashioned nuclear family is less and less able to provide children the material and emotional stability they need. . . . Some solutions we should consider: more public assistance for children; require (absent) fathers to contribute to their offspring, perhaps through the tax system; and an increase in federal funding for day care."

The importance of such pronouncements, echoed in most of the economic justice statements under discussion, cannot be overstated. They challenge the religious right's monopoly on family issues, and refute the notion that a "pro-family" agenda is one that reverses the trend of mothers into the workforce, crusades against funding for abortion *and* child care, eliminates social programs like AFDC that "interfere" with families, and focuses on such pressing family issues as pornography and school prayer. Instead, the religious economic justice advocates argue convincingly that the American family is changing in response to economic, not moral forces, and that a moral public policy helps families cope with those forces more effectively.

The Role of Government

All of the economic justice statements examined in this volume insist that a just economy requires a higher level of government spending, intervention and leadership—a contention that contradicts the common wisdom that government must shrink its efforts in the face of enormous budget deficits. But secure in their status as moral, not political leaders, religious groups were able to do what few politicians could bring themselves to do: criticize the tax-cutting frenzy that has drained the U.S. Treasury in the 1980s.

The Reagan administration's 1981 tax cut was a creative— some might say devious—device to impose its anti-government agenda by fiat. Rather than debate the merits of social spending and individual government programs, the administration pushed through a drastic tax cut that reversed the political equation, and forced social programs to justify their continued existence in the face of looming budget deficits. And few politicians of either major party have been willing to call for reversing the Reagan tax giveaway.

Caring for the casualties of that ideological assault, community religious leaders were among the first to fight back. Jacqueline Levine of the National Jewish Community Relations Advisory Council put it forcefully: "Even though opinion polls indicate that a majority of Americans are not averse to tax raises to cope with the deficits, and even though economists indicate that raising taxes to cope with them would not harm the economy, our nation's leadership is locked into an ideological political position masquerading as economics which refuses to recognize that choices exist." The Presbyterians called the nation's tax policies "an abomination to us as Christians" and concluded: "We've got to raise taxes—which means we Presbyterians are going to pay more."

As they outlined new priorities in the economic sphere, religious groups were strengthened by their long-standing concern about American military and foreign policy. The 1970s and 1980s saw a boom in religious activism against nuclear weapons and Central American intervention. When it came time to critique the spending priorities that hamper the government's ability to cure the economic ills they diagnosed, the Reagan administration's $300 billion military budget was a natural target. Almost every statement discussed in this volume contains a call to redirect resources from weaponry to social programs, a call that is justified on both domestic and foreign policy grounds. With two-thirds of the world's population living in poverty, several of the statements label it indefensible that the American defense budget is twenty times its foreign aid budget—and that within those figures all but a fraction of the foreign aid is military.

But even as religious groups ponder what public policy should do to foster a more just economy, their toughest challenge is facing the prevailing skepticism that there is anything they can do about poverty, unemployment, family stress, environmental degradation or any of the myriad social ills that afflict our society. Typical of the enormous social pessimism of the 1980s is Charles Murray's *Losing Ground,* which argues that Great Society welfare programs have in fact worsened poverty by providing an alternative to self-supporting work. But the religious economic justice movement unequivocally rejects the notion that "the government that governs least governs best," as the Catholic bishops describe it. Their goal has been to revive belief in collective action toward shared social goals, a radical notion in the individualistic Reagan era.

A Changing Climate

But if religious groups felt like prophets in the wilderness when they began to craft their economic justice messages, there is today a growing audience for their moral, social and political calls to action. Concern over scandal in Washington, takeovers and insider trading on Wall Street, environmental disasters here and around the globe, and poverty that has worsened in a time of economic growth—these and other indications strongly suggest that the headlines of the late 1980s are the precursors of change in the 1990s.

Newsweek proclaimed "the end of greed" at the close of 1987, and the beginning of a new era of altruism. Gallup polls showed a trend toward voluntarism; the number of people who gave of their time in community or charitable efforts rose thirteen percent between 1986 and 1988. But like the religious communities at the decade's start, as more people faced growing demands for their time, money and compassion, they recognized the limits of charity and began to support, at least theoretically, expanded government efforts to combat social problems. In the last two years polls have consistently shown support for tax hikes, especially if the new revenues are used for education, health, and children's programs such as day care.

In this changing climate, the religious economic justice movement has a broader constituency than many would have expected when it began. Now its challenge is to help that constituency build the long-lasting foundations of a more just economy, to ensure that economic justice is an enduring feature of American life, not merely a notion that moves in and out of fashion with the pendulum swings of American politics.

In the next three chapters we will examine statements by the three major religious groups in this country—Catholic, Protestant and Jewish—in response to the social realities that have just been described.

PART II

RESPONDING TO THE SITUATION: AN ANALYSIS OF MAJOR STATEMENTS BY RELIGIOUS BODIES

3. A New Catholic Voice on Social Issues

John A. Coleman, S.J.

The American Catholic bishops issued their influential document, "Economic Justice for All: Catholic Social Teaching and the U.S. Economy," in 1986. Three years earlier, the Canadian bishops upset (some said, "intruded upon") the Canadian political debate with their pastoral letter, "Ethical Reflections on the Economic Crisis."

Confronted with these two events, many commentators have wondered aloud, "Why this new Catholic voice on social issues?"

A Long Tradition of Social Concerns

In 1991, worldwide Catholicism will celebrate a hundred years of Catholic "social encyclicals," beginning with Pope Leo XIII's letter, *Rerum Novarum* in 1891, which endorsed the labor movement's struggle for unions and a just wage. In that first modern Catholic social charter, Leo stated:

> When there is a question of defending the rights of individuals, the poor and badly-off have a claim to especial consideration. The richer class have many ways of shielding themselves . . . whereas the mass of the poor must chiefly depend upon the assistance of the state.

Forty years later, Pope Pius XI added to this corpus of Catholic social thought with his 1931 encyclical, *Quadragesimo Anno*. Writing during the great depression, Pius XI deplored

31

monopoly capitalism and the replacement of a free market by economic domination. The pope brought a cautious suspicion to bear on both capitalism and socialism. He approved, under certain conditions, the nationalization of basic industries to serve the common good.

Reflecting on the church's critical attitude toward both liberal capitalism and Marxist collectivism, Ricardo Antoncich notes in his commentary on Catholic social teaching, *Christians in the Face of Injustice* (Orbis Books, Maryknoll, 1987), "Not only the Marxist ideology but the liberal as well—*and I mean the system itself and not simply the abuses of it (which might be corrected)*—call for great caution."

All the popes of the present century—notably John XXIII, Paul VI, and John Paul II—have added their distinctive contributions and updating to Catholic social thought.

Nor was the American bishops' letter of 1986 their first attempt to address economic issues. In 1919 they issued the provocative "Bishops' Program on Social Reconstruction" to address American post-war economic adjustments. Again, in 1940 and 1976 the American bishops issued major pastorals underscoring three persistent Catholic themes: (1) *A championing of the common good,* which means more than just the sum of disparate individual interests and common preferences. The common good *structures* society around notions and institutions that guarantee distributive justice, equality, and the claims of the needy. This common good undercuts purely utilitarian trade-offs or false individualism. (2) *A call to solidarity with the labor movement.* The bishops embrace unions, the right to strike, a just wage, and worker co-ownership and determination in industry. (3) *A recognition of the right to private property,* which includes a wide dispersion of property ownership. Moreover, as John Paul II states, "There is a social mortgage on all private property." The right to private property intends a collective good, however. The goods of the earth were created to serve all. Individual ownership and use of property makes sense only if it furthers this original creative purpose.

New Elements in Catholic Social Teaching Since
Vatican Council II

Despite this long history of Catholic social thought (which, of course, extends back beyond 1891 to the earliest times in the life of the church), there exist truly new elements in the tradition since Vatican Council II (1962–1965). It is possible, then, to speak of "a new Catholic voice in social issues." Seven of these elements provide background to the American and Canadian bishops' letters of the 1980s.

1. *A new humanism.* Catholic social thought has always been open to dialogue with non-Christian wisdom. An older understanding of "natural law" assumed that fundamental truths about economic justice and a social good could be known by all men and women of good will. Unfortunately, early Catholic "natural law" thought often saw society as a pre-ordained static order, untouched by historical development.

At Vatican II, however, especially in the document on "The Church in the Modern World" (#55), the Catholic bishops argued that creating a just society is a human project, discerned in the struggles for justice in history. Human beings are defined, above all, by their joint responsibility for history and one another. The "natural law" on this reading is dynamic; it unfolds in history and demands that Catholics cooperate with other Christians, Jews, and men and women of good will.

Since John XXIII, the papal social encyclicals have addressed themselves not just to Catholics but to "all persons of good will." Catholics recognize a rightful autonomy to the temporal order. If popes make ethical judgments about economic and political systems, they do not pretend to have some "Catholic blueprint" for just economies. The common good is a joint social project. Dialogue and the consensus of all citizens concerned for a common good characterize this new political humanism. While the church goes public with its ethical wisdom in its social teaching, it must at the same time respect the nature of a public and pluralistic common good.

2. *A liberationist perspective.* Since the late 1960s, influential bishops and theologians, mainly from Latin America, have criticized taking the advanced industrial nations as the unique model for economic development, since they signal a subtle (or not so subtle) neo-colonialism in the world market economy, so that the poor remain dependent on the rich. Since Vatican II, Catholic social thought speaks of "the signs of the times," secular trends of hope or despair, of improvements or failures in justice arrangements, which call for gospel corrective or approval. It points to the emancipatory movements of social justice and human rights as signs of hope for a more just economic order, and calls upon Catholics to show solidarity with these movements. Moreover, this new tradition places great emphasis on the so-called "north-south debate" about a more just world trade, aid, transfer of technology, and debt policy.

Catholic thought insists, following Pope Paul VI in his 1967 encyclical, *Populorum Progressio:* "Today the principal fact that we must all recognize is that the social question has become worldwide." A liberationist perspective underscores interdependence of economies, and calls for wide-reaching structural reforms in the world market. This view distrusts (as John Paul II underscores in his recent encyclical, *Sollicitudo Rei*) those who would systematically subordinate the north-south debate to the power conflicts between the east-west blocs, or totally reduce justice to security concerns.

3. *A social structural dimension to sin.* Since Vatican II, popes and bishops refer to the classic Christian notion of sin in social and structural terms. When sin is seen uniquely as an individual failing, it can be overcome by individual moral change, a conversion of the heart. But when sin is understood in structural terms, liberation from sin involves structural as well as moral change and conversion. In his new encyclical, John Paul II states the relation between individual and structural sin:

> Structures of sin . . . are rooted in personal sin and thus always linked to the concrete acts of individuals who introduce these structures, consolidate them and make them difficult to remove. And thus they grow stronger,

spread and become the source of other sins, and so influence people's behavior. (#36)

The pope cites examples of structural sin rooted in cultural distortions (e.g. consumerism as a way of life) as well as instances in economic structures (e.g. systemic unemployment or homelessness). Liberation from sin calls for a change of structures as well as a change of heart.

4. *A new openness to socialism.* Catholic social thought has long distrusted most forms of socialism because of their antireligious bias, their over-exaggerated sense of class conflict which verges on hatred of the enemy, their notion of economic determinism which denies that history remains open to human choices, and their substitution of a centralized bureaucracy for economic initiative and decentralized units for planning and economic action. Catholicism espouses instead a doctrine of *subsidiarity* (to be discussed later), which champions decentralization. Still, especially since Paul VI, the church's social teaching has refused to condemn socialism as a possible economic option. Indeed, in his ground-breaking 1981 encyclical on human work, *Laborem Exercens,* John Paul II took as his starting point the characteristic economic questions of socialism.

If the answers of Catholic social thought about the economic order differ from many versions of socialism (as they differ from most versions of capitalism), the tradition frequently agrees with the socialist analysis of the situation of injustice. Speaking of western liberal capitalism and Marxist collectivism, John Paul II states in his latest encyclical that "the church does not show preference for one or the other, provided that human dignity is properly respected and promoted" and religious freedom granted. The pope wants to avoid the manipulation of the church by those, frequently in our own country, who use its aura to legitimate the reigning capitalist economic system. The pope continues:

> The church's social doctrine is not a "third way" between liberal capitalism and Marxist collectivism. . . .
> Nor is it an ideology but rather the accurate formulation

of the results of a careful reflection on the complex realities of human existence, in society and in the international order, in the light of faith and of the church's tradition. Its main aim is to interpret these realities, determining their conformity with or divergence from the lines of the gospel teaching on the human person and his vocation. . . . Its aim is thus to guide Christian behavior. (#41)

Catholic social thought, in this view, must combine careful social analysis with gospel judgment. Neither alone will suffice.

5. *A preferential option for the poor.* In biblical thought, the litmus test for any society consists in the way it treats widows, orphans, alien farm workers—in short, the poor—in its midst. In the teaching of Jesus, the poor are called "God's poor," and to meet the poor is to meet Christ. Even the medieval church countered the right to private property with the "rights of the poor." First strongly enunciated by the Latin American bishops in their meeting at Puebla, Mexico, in 1979, this biblical idea of "a preferential option for the poor" has become firmly grafted onto Catholic social thought. Pope John Paul II has endorsed it, as have the American and Canadian bishops. Hence, when the American bishops look at the U.S. economy, they state:

> Decisions must be judged in the light of what they do *for* the poor, what they do *to* the poor, and what they enable the poor to do *for themselves*. The fundamental moral criterion for all economic decisions, policies and institutions is this: they must be at the service *of all people, especially the poor.* (#24)

6. *The priority of labor over capital.* In his 1981 encyclical on work, John Paul II enunciates a Catholic version of the labor theory of value. He stresses, first, that "the basis for determining the value of human work is not primarily the kind of work being done, but the fact that the one doing it is a person. . . . In the first place work is 'for man' and not man 'for work.' " (#6) The

prime error in early capitalism (and later socialism), in the pope's view,

> can be repeated wherever the human person is in a way treated on the same level as the whole complex of the material means of production, as an instrument, and not in accordance with the true dignity of his or her work —that is to say, where he or she is not treated as subject and maker, and for this very reason as the true purpose of the whole process of production. (#7)

Finally, against every reduction of persons to things, John Paul asserts the priority of labor over capital:

> We must emphasize and give prominence to the primacy of the human in the production process, the primacy of persons over things. Everything contained in the concept of capital, in the strict sense, is only a collection of things. Humans, as the subject of work and independent of work, in all that they do—humans alone are persons. (#12)

The pope expands the narrow Marxist notion of work to include the entrepreneur, the artist, the business manager. All have their place in the economy. Ultimately, the final judge of an economy is not an impersonal, technical criterion, but a personal judgment about what the economy does to the workers in it.

The American bishops were very conscious of John Paul's principle of the priority of labor over capital when they wrote their pastoral. Hence, they begin with three questions that reflect this priority:

> Every perspective on economic life that is human, moral and Christian must be shaped by three questions: What does the economy do *for* people? What does it do *to* people? And how do people *participate* in it? The economy is a human reality: men and women working to-

gether to develop and care for the whole of God's creation. All this work must serve the material and spiritual well-being of people. (#1)

(We have already seen that the bishops ask the same questions about the poor.) And if this is what the economy is, in its essential reality—the human reality of men and women working together to develop the goods of our earth—then ordinary men and women have a legitimate say about the development of the economy. They cannot leave it just to the experts.

7. *A new contextualism.* A final new element in Catholic social thought since Vatican II can be called a new contextualism. Each national church must address its own social and economic context, taking the wider Catholic social teaching's principles and applying them with bite and impact in their own context. Thus, the Brazilian bishops address justice issues connected with land development in the Amazon where large multinational firms drive small farmers from their ancestral land, or the Canadian bishops assess Canada's giant oil development projects in the northwest which displace the Indian tribes and cause environmental destruction. The charter for this new contextualism is Pope Paul VI's pastoral letter, *Octogesima Adveniens:*

> It is up to the Christian communities to analyze with objectivity the situation which is proper to their own country, to shed on it the light of the gospel's unalterable words and to draw principles of reflection, norms of judgment and directives for action from the social teaching of the church. (#4)

The American Bishops' Letter on the Economy

In the American Catholic letter on the economy, the bishops seek to take the above advice of Paul VI seriously and to provide "principles of reflection, norms of judgment and directives for action" in the American context.

Before announcing their principles of reflection, the bishops first state *why* they speak to the issue of the American economy.

This church in its pastoral ministry sees every day the faces of the poor, of young people struggling for jobs, of new immigrants, of conscientious business people seeking new and more equitable ways to organize resources and the workplace. The economy enters the rectories of parishes in homeless persons asking for a place to sleep, in hungry persons asking for food, in unemployed persons seeking resources to find work. Moreover, the bishops themselves are managers of complex economic systems including schools, hospitals, and agencies of charity outreach. Churches are investors and employers in the American system, and cannot be excluded from the discussions about the directions the American economy might take.

They assert the need to bring *an ethical perspective* to any discussion of the economy and new economic policies:

> Economic arrangements can be sources of fulfillment, of hope, of community—or of frustration, isolation and even despair. They teach virtues—or vices—and day by day help mold our characters. They affect the quality of people's lives; at the extreme, even determining whether people live or die. Serious economic choices go beyond merely technical issues to fundamental questions of value and human purpose. (#5)

Theirs is a new humanism that seeks "an ethical framework that can guide economic life today in ways that are both faithful to the gospel and shaped by human experience and reason." (#61) They look to dialogue and consensus with the wider public for "in the absence of a vital sense of citizenship among the businesses, corporations, labor unions and other groups that shape economic life, society as a whole is endangered." (#66) They root their hope for structural renewal in "our belief that the country can attain a renewed moral vision." (#27)

Five basic principles govern the bishops' moral assessment of the U.S. economy:

1. *The principle of human dignity.* "The principle of the dignity of the human person, realized in community with others, is the criterion against which all aspects of economic life must be

measured." (#28) Human dignity is both personal and communal. Personal dignity flows from the creation of all humans in the image of God. Communal dignity is rooted in the biblical concept of a *covenant,* which is more than a mere utilitarian *contract,* since it entails a relationship with God, with others in such extra-contractual relationships as mercy and compassion, and with the earth's resources.

2. *The principle of solidarity.* Human life is life in community (#63). Thus:

> What the Bible and Christian tradition teach, human wisdom confirms. Centuries before Christ the Greeks and Romans spoke of the human person as a 'social animal,' made for friendship, community and public life. These insights show that human beings achieve self-realization not in isolation but in interaction with others. (#65)

So the bishops endorse neither rugged individualism as a cultural virtue, nor the mindless tolerance of "do your own thing."

3. *The principle of justice and participation.* Here the bishops employ traditional but important distinctions: (a) *"Commutative justice* calls for fundamental fairness in all agreements and exchanges between individuals or private social groups." (#69) Workers owe their employers diligent work; employers owe their workers a fair wage and humane conditions of work. (b) *"Distributive justice* requires that the allocation of income, wealth and power in society be evaluated by its effects on persons whose basic material needs are unmet." (#70) Basic human needs take preference over superfluous wants and luxury preferences. (c) *"Social justice* implies that persons have an obligation to be active and productive participants in the life of society and that society has a duty to enable them to participate in this way." (#71)

Thus the bishops champion a version of economic democracy that would bring together the best of our American political and economic wisdom. Theirs is a radical proposal. We cannot leave the economy simply to technical experts, although they have a legitimate role to play. Justice itself, the bishops are saying, calls for a society in which *all* share in the decision-making. "Basic justice demands the establishment of minimum levels of participation in the life of the human society for all persons." (#76) This leads directly to the next principle.

4. *The principle of "the preferential option for the poor."* The principle, which we have already encountered, is best put in the bishops' own words:

> The prime purpose of this special commitment to the poor is to enable them to become active participants in the life of society. It is to enable *all* persons to share in and contribute to the common good. The option for the poor, therefore, is not an adversarial slogan that pits one group or class against another. Rather it states that the deprivation and powerlessness of the poor wounds the whole community. The extent of their suffering is a measure of how far we are from being a true community of persons. (#87)

5. *The principle of subsidiarity.* The bishops do not endorse a statist economy. They follow Catholic thought in championing initiatives by voluntary groups in the private sector, such as business, unions, and local community groups. The state is not the whole of society, nor has it a monopoly on defining the common good. Still, subsidiarity—a bias toward local initiative and intermediary groups between the state and the individual—must be counter-balanced. "The teachings of the church insist that government has a moral function: protecting the human rights and securing basic justice for all members of the commonwealth." (#119) Catholic thought is not preoccupied with "getting government off our backs," nor does it subscribe to the notion that "that government is best which governs least." On the contrary, government has a moral responsibility to make sure the common good of justice for all is achieved.

Using these five basic principles, the bishops turn to selected economic policy issues: unemployment, poverty, food and agriculture, and the impact of the U.S. economy on developing nations. Here the bishops move from overall principles and norms to specific directives for action. For example: "Vigorous action should be undertaken to remove barriers to full and equal employment for women and minorities," (#196) since poverty and unemployment fall unequally on them. Again: "The tax system must be reformed to reduce the burden on the poor." (#199) And again: "Moderate sized farms operated by families on a full-time basis should be preserved and their economic viability protected." (#230)

It is important to note that, before writing their letter, the bishops held hearings at which economists, business and union leaders, welfare mothers, community organizers, and many others testified to what the economy was doing for, to—and against— people. James Tobin, Nobel Prize winner in economics, has stated that the bishops got their economics right because they provided a forum where representatives of *all* the voices in the land could be heard. But in their letter, the bishops carefully state that when they move from general principles to directions for action (relying on social science data), their teaching authority diminishes and is more open to debate and dissent. This is consistent with their acknowledgement of a rightful autonomy to the temporal and technical, so long as the latter does not become an amoral determinism.

Throughout the letter the aim is not only "to provide guidance for members of our own church as they seek to form their consciences about economic matters," but also to influence a larger public debate and discussion about the ethical quality of American economic life:

> We want to add our voice to the public debate about the directions in which the U.S. economy should be moving. We seek the cooperation and support of those who do not share our faith or tradition. . . . The questions are basic and the answers often elusive, but it is now time for serious and sustained attention to economic justice. (#27)

Canada vs. the United States

The Canadian Catholic bishops, to whom reference was made at the beginning of this chapter, also want to contribute to "serious and sustained attention to economic justice." Rather than issuing one long and technical document on the economy, Canada's bishops have contributed to the Canadian economic discussion with a sustained series of reflections spanning more than fifteen years, on such topics as "Sharing Nation Income" (1972), "On Decent Housing for All" (1976), "Social Ethical Guidelines for Investment" (1979), "Toward a New International Economic Order" (1981), "Ethical Reflections on the Economic Crisis" (1982) and "Defending Workers' Rights: A New Frontier" (1985). (See E.F. Sheridan, ed., *Do Justice,* Sherbrooke, Quebec, Les Éditions Paulines, 1987, for this collection of letters.)

Like the U.S. bishops, the Canadians root their thought and reflections in earlier consultations with their people. They differ from their U.S. counterparts, however, in asserting "a much larger structural crisis in the international system of capitalism," and underscoring that social justice involves a struggle, even a conflict, in society. They also place great stress, beyond reformist tinkering, in facing alternative possibilities:

> What would it mean to develop an alternative economic model that would place emphasis on: socially useful forms of production; labour-intensive industries; self-reliant models of economic development; community ownership and control of industries; new forms of worker ownership and management; and greater use of the renewable energy sources in industrial production?

The Canadian priorities for ethical judgment are succinct and unequivocal:

> The needs of the poor have priority over the wants of the rich; the rights of workers are more important than the

maximization of profits; the preservation of marginalized groups has precedence over the preservation of a
system which excludes them.

(The history of these priority principles is quite interesting. They
were first coined by David Hollenbach, S.J. in a book on human
rights, *Claims in Conflict,* Paulist Press, 1979. Although he was
one of the principal drafters of the American letter on the economy, modesty kept Hollenbach from quoting his own maxims in
the American letter, although their spirit obviously pervades the
American bishops' reflections. In speeches made during his visit
to Canada, Pope Paul II adopted these principles as his own.)

Canada's bishops raise issues about the extent of foreign
ownership of Canadian industry, and, more generally, the unregu-
lated rule by multinational corporations whose wealth and power
surpass that of many sovereign states. They squarely face elements
of the third world in their own country, especially in parts of
Quebec and the Maritime Provinces, and address the flight of
industry and jobs through plant closings.

Canadian Catholic social teaching is more ecumenical than
in the United States. The Catholic bishops frequently issue joint
statements and engage in common action with other Canadian
churches. Moreover, speaking of socialism in Canada is not a
taboo, as it frequently appears to be in the United States, and
Canada has its own indigenous non-Marxist brand of socialism in
the NDF party, originally founded by Protestant social gospel
thinkers.

The Canadian bishops teach a fivefold *method* for devising
an appropriate church social teaching and action. We in the
American churches could learn from it:

(1) being present with and listening to the experience
of the poor, the marginalized, the oppressed in our society; (2) developing a critical analysis of the economic,
political and social structures that cause human suffering; (3) making judgments in the light of gospel principles and the social teachings of the church; (4)
stimulating creative thought and action regarding alter-

native visions and models for social and economic development; (5) acting in solidarity with popular groups in their struggles to transform economic, political and social structures.

The latter two principles go beyond anything found in the American bishops' letter.

Conclusion

The Canadian and American Catholic bishops, taking a lead from international Catholic social thought, want to stimulate and contribute to a renewal of active citizenship and economic justice in our countries and world. They want to add, not impose, their voices in a wider dialogue about the quality of national economic life and international community. There are no indications that this new Catholic voice on social issues will soon fall silent. But to move from principles and directives to action will take the creative imaginations and applications of people in the pews and at their work benches and business offices.

That dialogue—widespread and involving every strand of active citizenship upon which our countries depend—has barely begun.

4. Protestant Statements on Economic Justice

Karen Lebacqz

While the National Conference of Catholic Bishops was busy developing its statement on economic justice, a number of Protestant groups were moving in similar directions. [See appendix.] Of these, we will focus on six representative groups of statements: (1) the Disciples of Christ, "Economic Systems—Their Impact on the Third World: A Beginning Christian Study," (2) the Episcopal Church in the United States, "Economic Justice and the Christian Conscience" (prepared by the Urban Bishops Coalition), (3) the Lutheran Church in America (now part of the Evangelical Lutheran Church in America), "Economic Justice: Stewardship of Creation in Human Community," (4) the United Church of Christ, "Christian Faith and Economic Life," (5) the United Presbyterian Church, "Christian Faith and Economic Justice," and (6) the Church of the Brethren, "Christian Lifestyle" and "Justice and Nonviolence."

Each denominational statement reflects something of the distinctive character of that denomination. None are entirely similar to the statements from other denominations, yet five of the six—those from the Disciples, Episcopal, Lutheran, Presbyterian, and United Church of Christ churches—have enough in common that they can be classified as sharing a perspective that represents in broad brush strokes a mainline Protestant view. The sixth document, from the Church of the Brethren, represents the Anabaptist and more "sectarian" tradition, and will provide an alternative perspective helpful in posing questions to the mainline approach.

I. "Mainline Protestants"—A Common Approach

Typically, mainline statements offer a vision of justice, peace, or God's will, known primarily from biblical sources. This biblical base acts as a kind of picture of "what ought to be." From this vision, they then derive "yardsticks" for economic justice. These yardsticks or mandates are an attempt to refine and specify the ethical implications of the broader vision drawn above. They generally include the dignity of each person and the fundamental equality of persons, special concern for the poor or marginalized, a fundamental requirement to meet basic economic needs as being central to a just economy, and an understanding of community as central to human life and value.

Against this vision of a just or "shalom" community and its ethical requirements, a description of the present situation is posed. The documents suggest reasons for the development of the situation. Some include historical notes or particular examples of economic problems around the world. Several offer at least a brief review of different economic systems and how they work.

This juxtaposition of the Christian vision and yardsticks for economic justice with the current situation provides a basis for the judgment that the current situation constitutes a "crisis" involving injustices that must be corrected. Attention is given to proposed corrective measures, both for the social and economic order in general, and for particular groups such as governments and churches.

The basic approach, then, is to *judge current reality against a biblically-inspired picture of justice, in order to ground a judgment that injustice exists and to call for corrective action.* The specifics of this broad picture may differ a bit from denomination to denomination, but the root approach remains the same: comparison of a biblically-inspired picture to the current situation leading to judgments of wrong-doing and needed correctives.

II. A Biblical and Theological Vision

The biblical vision used to ground ethical judgments about the economy generally includes the following:

(1) *God cares about the material world and hence economics and faith cannot be separated:* "Since the Lord is Ruler of *all* life, the economic order in which we live cannot escape the careful scrutiny of faith." (UPCUSA #077; cf. LCA p. 2) Whether the theme is framed in the language of God as the great Economist (UCC #28) or simply in terms of multiple references to the rich and the poor in scripture, all agree that God seeks economic justice. This affirmation of God's concern for the material world provides a base for Christian attention to matters of economic justice.

(2) *Everything that is belongs to God:* "The earth is the Lord's." (LCA p. 1) From this basic affirmation follow several corollaries.

First, *no human has a "right" to anything outside of God's purposes for it.* For example, private property is not an absolute right: "humanity's access to resources, including ownership of private property, is conditional." (UCC #44)

Second, *humans are stewards:* "God's people are to behave like 'stewards'. . . ." (Episc. p. 8) The UCC notes that there are no fewer than twenty-six direct references to this concept in scripture. (UCC #43) Stewards are managers: "God is the owner; we are to manage creation for its Creator." (UPCUSA #085) Hence, stewardship implies accountability: "Scripture depicts humans as stewards or managers accountable to God for caring for the creation in accordance with God's intentions." (UCC #43) *Humans must take responsibility* for the economic situation of the world, including its injustices.

This responsibility implies first a prophetic role of judgment: we are to become "a conscious channel for God's judging word on those societal arrangements and economic decisions that cause pain and injustice." (Episc. p. 10) It implies second a pastoral role of caring for creation: "It is a betrayal of trust if we waste [creation] or abuse it or fail to pass it on in good condition to the next generation of God's children." (UPCUSA #085) Our role as stewards grounds our efforts to speak out and to act for economic justice.

(3) *Humans are made in God's image:* "We ourselves are created 'in the image of God' (Gen 1:27)." (UPCUSA #086; cf.

LCA pp. 1–2) This means that each person is of inestimable worth: "Humans are to be honored and respected with utmost seriousness." (UPCUSA #086). Being created in God's image can also mean that humans are "co-creators" with God (Episc. p. 13), and thus that human work takes on a special significance as a way of serving God (UCC #255), of self-expression and self-realization, and of contributing to the larger community. (UCC #63; here they refer directly to the NCCB)

(4) *God has a special concern for the poor and oppressed:* "Yahweh has a particular concern for those 'left out'. . . ." (Episc. p. 8, citing Dt 24:21) This concern is reflected throughout scripture: "The Bible is replete with references which emphasize a concern for the poor." (Disc. #38, citing Pss 10, 15, 35; Am 2:7; Lk 1:46–56, 1 Sam 2:8; Mt 25:35f) Several passages in particular are used as grounding for God's special concern for the poor and oppressed—the jubilee provisions and Jesus' pronouncement in Luke 4:18 of preaching good news to the poor and inaugurating the jubilee: "Living with and as one of the poor of his day, Jesus incarnated God's presence among and concern for the needy and alienated." (UCC #39, citing Lk 4:18; Mk 9:35; Lk 16:19f; Ex 23:6; Dt 15:7f; Dt 14:27; Lv 25:8f)[1]

(5) *We are created for community, for covenant:* "Life under God is also meant to be life in community." (LCA p. 2) God's covenants were with a people; Jesus called his disciples into community; the early church even practiced communal ownership. (Disc #40–41; cf. Episc. p. 9: "The 'kingdom' [Jesus] preached was at its core relational.") As each person is of inestimable worth, so also each person needs others in order to be fully human: "It is only together that persons can realize their creation in God's image." (LCA p. 2) There is no justice apart from community: "The Bible emphasizes the intrinsic need for persons to live in community in order to achieve fulfillment and well-being and to be faithful to God's intentions." (UCC #66) Indeed, some would go so far as to say that "the most apt description of the

---

1. It should be noted, however, that the LCA is conspicuously lacking in this emphasis, and in this regard deviates from the other mainline statements.

50 / *Karen Lebacqz*

Judeo/Christian community is that of a family." (Disciples #42; cf. LCA p. 2)

(6) However, while we are created in God's image and for community, *we are also sinful and fallen:* "Human pride and sinfulness through the ages have perverted the responsibility to care for the creation. . . ." (UCC #78) Our world is "broken by sin." (LCA p. 2; cf. UPCUSA #102: "The Bible affirms that all of us are sinners"; cf. Disc #47: "The Bible acknowledges the existence of human sin. . . .") The unjust steward of Luke 12:45–48 symbolizes "human beings throughout history whose disobedience, disloyalty, unfaithfulness, and apathy have distorted, disrupted, and undermined relationships with God, neighbors, and all of creation." (UCC #45) Moreover, "the prophets make clear that in a society divided along the lines of power and privilege, not only active oppression but complacent neglect, is sin." (UPCUSA #062)

Sinfulness takes the form both of idolatry (false belief and the worship of false gods) and of selfishness (injustice, covetousness). (Disc. #47) Sin is exhibited both in personal sins and in structural or social sin, embodied in systems and policies. (UCC #46; cf. UPCUSA #104; LCA p. 3)

III. Ethical Mandates

From these basic theological affirmations flow certain *ethical presuppositions and standards:*

(1) *Justice requires equal respect for all:* "Because the God of justice gives equal and irreducible value to every person, we are required in justice to show equal concern and respect for every person." (UPCUSA #212) "Stated as a positive rule, all human beings deserve respect and are entitled to develop their full potential." (Disc. #45)

For several groups, equal respect for all is demonstrated in the affirmation of certain basic human rights or entitlements. The UCC argues for a "positive conception" of basic rights including food and water, health care, housing, meaningful employment, education, participation, protection from torture, and non-discrimination. (#75) The Disciples include as basic economic rights freedom from: hunger, poverty, lack of medical care, homelessness, and joblessness. (#45) The Episcopalians pose a "divine right" of access to food, shelter, medical care, freedom, and a chance to participate. (p. 2)

(2) *Justice requires special concern for the poor and oppressed:* Concern for the poor is "not a matter of private inclination to charity" but is a "demand of God." (UPCUSA #047; cf. #091: "God's special concern for the poor and the powerless make[s] our attitudes toward and actions for them a test of our loyalty to God.") The implication of God's special concern for the poor is clear, suggest the Disciples: "A Christian will require any economic system to give an account of how it will improve the lot of the poor." (Disc. #39) The UCC concurs: "A major criterion for a faith-centered economics is whether particular institutions and policies enhance the life opportunities of the poor, the weak, and the groups at the margins of society. This mandate represents a contemporary application of Jesus' ministry of incarnating God's presence." (UCC #55)

For most groups, concern for the poor means minimally that justice requires responding to need: "a just economic system fulfills the basic material needs of all members of the human community." (UCC #52; they draw here on the parable of the great judgment in Mt 25:31–46) Concern for the poor also means enabling the poor to be full participants in society: while the LCA generally lacks a focus on the poor, it does suggest that in the mode of "equity," justice requires both response to need and providing for those minimal necessities that are prerequisites for participation in society. (LCA p. 6) In some documents, it is not merely a matter of meeting needs or providing the necessities for participation, but of actively attempting to enter the lives of the poor and standing with them: "We should attempt to enter into the pain of those who are poor or afflicted and to stand with them in their struggle for justice." (Episc. p. 8)

(3) *Just economic systems build community, create harmony:* "The doctrine of God's love teaches that we are created for *community*. Justice is a *community* concept." (UPCUSA #131) Indeed, community comes first and sets the stage for economics: "In our contemporary situation, if we seek first to create

the community of those who love God and neighbor, we will then know what it is we want our economy to produce." (Episc. p. 9) Hence, economies are to serve communities: "Economic life is not an end in itself but instead a means by which human communities can be built and people's lives enriched." (UCC #70)

Recognition that humans are communal beings means that Christians will be "critical of those aspects of an economic system marked by division and antagonism, unconcerned with the lives people share with one another." (Disc. #43) "Humankind is a single family so that all economic questions and problems are to be understood as among brothers and sisters." (UPCUSA #089) Discriminatory attitudes and practices therefore constitute "an affront to the Christian affirmation of the equality and worth of all human beings and the inclusiveness of the community." (UCC #69; cf. LCA p. 7: Arrangements that exclude and stigmatize people are "a double affront to the Creator and to persons created in God's image.") Hence, "those economic conditions that thwart full participation or that generate inequality and injustice therefore are as odious as despotic rulers." (UCC #60)

By implication, justice requires that all are able to *participate:* "A just economic system is inclusive, involving all people in responsible, participatory, and economically rewarding activity." (UCC #60) Justice requires respect for the decision-making powers of people: "Members of a society should be co-determiners of the quality of their economic life." (LCA p. 6) "One way in which Christians evaluate an economy is by the opportunities it affords all for the responsible use of liberty." (UPCUSA #130)

(4) *Justice will require not simply good intentions, but structural protections against sin:* "For Christians the recognition of the reality of sin calls for building into our political and economic systems what Luther called 'dykes against sin'—protections to guard against the selfish abuses of power (whether private or public) which conflict with the public interest or the common good." (UPCUSA #107; cf. LCA p. 4) For some, the very concept of justice is such a protection, since it implies demands that transcend individual good will.

IV. Defining the Situation

Drawing on these biblical, theological, and ethical premises, all would agree upon certain approaches to the current situation. (1) *We face an economic crisis.* (UCC #12–13; UPCUSA #153) Indicators of this crisis or trouble include: inflation, unemployment, the feminization of poverty, racial discrimination, defaulting on loans, hunger, dwindling resources and environmental damage, militarization and the arms race, and especially the gap between rich and poor. (UPCUSA #144–151; cf. Episc. pp. 4–7; UCC chapters 6 and 7; LCA p. 2) Various statistics are given on poverty, unemployment, discrimination, and particularly on the gap between rich and poor: "The world continues to be divided between the one-third who are affluent and the two-thirds who are poor." (UCC #11)

(2) *This crisis constitutes a moral outrage.* (UCC #10) Hunger in the midst of plenty is "appalling" (UCC #11); "An arrangement of radical insufficiency cannot go unchallenged if the concern for justice is to be met." (UPCUSA #226) "When there are food surpluses in North America and Western Europe and people starving in other parts of the world, something is horribly wrong." (UCC #144) "Christians can never be satisfied with a world that can produce food for all but in which millions suffer from malnutrition." (Disc. #147) "Vast disparities of income and wealth are both divisive of the human community and demeaning to its members." (LCA p. 7)

As a moral outrage, the situation cannot be permitted to continue: "We see much that we must condemn, confess our complicity with, repent of, and seek to change." (UPCUSA #228) "Deliverance. For both rich and poor that word may not be too strong a term to describe the national and global need today." (Episc. p. 1)

(3) *Economic problems and injustices are systemic, not simply individual.* "Social sin, embodied in systems and structures, can harm whole sectors of society: the poor, racial, ethnic, and religious minorities, women." (UCC #46) That is, sin is structured into the very systems that were originally intended to

do good. "The conclusion to which we are driven by our sense of the justice that God requires is that even if it does not involve anyone's *doing* anything wrong, any system that permits needless starvation is morally objectionable and offensive to God." (UPCUSA #227) For this reason, "quick fix" or "band-aid" remedies will not do. (Episc. p. 1, p. 12; cf. Disc. #15)

(4) *There will be no peace without economic justice.* "True security for the people demands respect for human rights, including the right of self-determination, as well as social and economic justice for all within every nation. . . ." (Disc. #3; cf. UCC #83) Thus, economic justice is central to world peace and related issues today.

(5) *A global perspective on the problem is necessary.* As important as it may be to "begin at home," it is not sufficient to worry about economic justice within the United States alone. Our economic system is too intricately interwoven with global questions: "A central fact of the contemporary situation is that a global economy already exists." (Disc. #7; cf. UCC: "We all live today as part of a global economy," #81) "The almost universal dependence on trade for the acquisition of essential raw materials and the securing of markets makes virtually all countries vulnerable to changes in international economic trends and the occurrence of economic disruptions." (UCC #125) Indeed, several documents discuss the interrelationships of economies at some length. (see UCC chapter 5 on "The Emergence of a Global Economy"; also their discussion of global poverty #167–180; UPCUSA chapter 2: "The Global Economic Situation . . ."; however, note also that the global discussion is missing from the LCA) Thus, "American poverty must . . . be seen in the context of immense economic pain abroad." (Episc. p. 6; the UCC quote the "open letter" from third world Christian churches in 1978 (UCC #15–16) and they also discuss dependency theory) In this context, revolutions taking place among the poor and oppressed can be seen as signs of hope. (UPCUSA #231)

(6) *The root of the problem may be described as ideological:* "An ideology can be . . . used deceptively to mask injustice and to elicit an ultimate commitment which, besides being idolatrous, may make people insensitive to the violation of basic

human rights.'' (LCA p. 5) That is, our world-view is central to both problem and solution. The development of a ''money culture'' (Episc. p. 6), a ''win-lose'' mentality (UCC #292), our tendency ''to spend an inordinate amount of time and energy in economic pursuits'' (UPCUSA #079)—these are seen as the crucial problems that must be addressed. In short, at root the problem is a moral and theological one: ''We believe our economic problems persist not so much because of fiscal imponderables as because we lack the moral will as a people to reorder our value priorities.'' (Episc. p. 15)

V. Solutions

These definitions of the situation become the basis for proposed solutions.

(1) Because the problem is at root ideological, the solution also involves *embracing a new ideology:* ''In the long run, only a major re-orienting of society's operational values can make possible the laying of a new foundation on which a truly just economy can thrive.'' (Episc. p. 1) The beginning point is ''a new vision of economics in which God is at the center, not at the periphery or excluded altogether.'' (UCC #244; cf. also #202–204) How we think is central: ''The refinement of appropriate concepts is a vital part of the constructive work of seeking justice.'' (LCA p. 4)

(2) One of the central values to be embraced is a *willingness to critique all economic systems.* Because of our capacity for sin, all systems are suspect. Therefore ''Christians will be critical of all economic systems'' (Disc. #49) which ''must be evaluated by the just standards of God's kingdom.'' (UPCUSA #080; cf. UCC #32)

When judged by kingdom standards, ''No current economic system fulfills the biblical mandates for economic justice.'' (UCC #290) None of the Protestant documents takes a strong stand in suggesting which economic system is best, but most subject both capitalism and socialism to criticism. (Disc. #99–106; Episc. p. 3; UPCUSA #080) Indeed, the UCC goes so far as to call capitalism, socialism and communism ''materialistic heresies'' because they subordinate other human values to ''the imperatives of eco-

nomic production." (UCC #290) While noting that all economies are mixed (UPCUSA #242), the Presbyterians argue that
both laissez-faire capitalism and Marxist communism have "fatal
flaws" (#251) that should keep us from embracing either whole-
heartedly: capitalism too often fails to provide for the poor
(#292), while socialism fails to provide adequately for liberty
and neglects important aspects of sin (#293).

(3) While no system is given unqualified support, all agree
that *economic systems cannot be judged by growth or productivity alone.* "Christians are first to ask of the economic system
not whether it is most efficient or productive of economic goods,
as important as that is, but how it reflects the purpose of God for
creation." (UPCUSA #081) "Scripture underscores the need to
evaluate economic systems on broader grounds in addition to, or
other than, productivity or efficiency." (UCC #54) "Productivity, in [Jesus'] view, is only a means, even if an important means,
to this larger end [of establishing a beloved community]." (Episc.
p. 9) Thus, for example, the Disciples propose that "employ-
ment/unemployment statistics offer another perspective for evaluating economic systems." (Disc. #55)

(4) *All are agreed, at least by implication, that governments carry some special responsibility to alleviate problems
of poverty and work for economic justice.* Some are explicit
about this: "In a sinful world God intends the institutions of
government to be the means of enforcing the claims of economic
justice." (LCA p. 5) "We submit that government at all levels
must [be] challenged once again to play a responsible role in
correcting the inequities in the economic crisis." (Episc. p. 14;
cf. p. 14: "This responsibility through government cannot be
overstressed.")

Others are less explicit but seem to imply that government is
a key actor in the economic arena and therefore a key focus for
change—e.g., the UCC speaks of a "society" willing to relin-
quish its advantages (#297) and calls for the adoption of a specific economic "bill of rights" as an amendment to the
Constitution (#205), the Disciples discuss various national policies and experiences in reviewing entire economic systems
(#66–98) and talk about the role of "superpower" nations

(#133). Such discussions of entire systems imply that change must be structural and therefore is the responsibility of governments.

As a corollary, Christians are urged to become involved politically: "By political activity we can protest what is unjust and work with others toward a better society, thereby responding to God's call to serve the cause of justice." (UPCUSA #342)

(5) However, *churches also have an important role.* That role takes several forms. One is witness: "The way in which the church acts as steward of its own resources is critical." (UCC #269) Another is judgment: "We should focus God's judging word on oppression wherever we discern it. . . ." (Episc. p. 8) Another is direct action: "We must never overlook the importance of the church becoming involved in direct ministries of compassion to those in critical need." (UPCUSA #327) "We should help to rebuild a sense of community . . ." and "to enter into the pain of those who are poor or afflicted and to stand with them in their struggle for justice." (Episc. p. 8) There is also an educational role: "We need to learn as much as we can about what is going on in the world." (UPCUSA #320) "We should labor at recovering a renewed theology of 'work'." (Episc. p. 8) Finally, there is advocacy: "We will want to advocate [our chosen] approach and debate its merits. . . ." (Disc. #150) Thus, churches are seen as having both prophetic and pastoral roles in response to the vision of justice and the gap between vision and reality.

VI. An Alternative Approach

When we turn from the mainline Protestant approach to the statements of the Church of the Brethren, we find many similarities but some striking and suggestive differences.

The Brethren share with their Protestant neighbors many basic theological and ethical affirmations. They agree that the earth is God's and that humans are "stewards." (Lifestyle pp. 8, 10–11; cf. their 1985 annual conference statement on "Christian Stewardship: Responsible Freedom") They agree that sin is evident and that it exists because of systems, not simply because of individual malice. (Justice pp. 4–5) They affirm that humans are basically social (Justice 9), that all people should be respected (Justice pp. 4–5), that there are basic rights such as food (Justice p. 9), and that the poor should be protected (Justice pp. 4–5). They also concur in much of the definition of the current problem and its solutions: that maldistribution of world resources is a serious problem (Lifestyle p. 11), that the profit motive is not sufficient as a measure of economic systems (Lifestyle p. 8), that problems must be dealt with on an international level (Justice p. 6), and that the "good life" is not made up of material luxuries and hence ideology is central (Lifestyle p. 8).

Yet for all these similarities, there are striking differences in tone, emphasis, and approach. First, the primary concern of the Brethren is for the role of the church and its people—how we should "live" as Christians. Other denominations also include attention to the role of the church. But often it is the last section of a paper otherwise devoted to social policy in general. In the Church of the Brethren, there is a strong emphasis on "getting one's own house in order first." Concern for Christian lifestyle is not a secondary concern nor complementary to political efforts, but is the primary concern.

Second, within this concern there are distinctive emphases. Other church groups also counsel "simple living" or reductions in wealth for Christians. But the Brethren urge not merely prayer and involvement but concrete actions such as adopting a graduated tithe, investing only in certain banks, and so on. (Lifestyle p. 5)

Moreover, the Brethren put particular emphasis on *the use of power* as a central issue. They utilize the same Lukan passage (4:18f) that undergirds other groups' emphasis on the poor, but rather than simply discussing the need to "help" the poor or to "stand with" the poor, their focus is on their own complicity in oppressive systems. (Lifestyle p. 9) They eschew worldly power as the proper means to correct problems: "As participants in a kingdom which seeks the lost, redeems the outcast, liberates the captives, and proclaims the redistribution of wealth and property in the jubilee year of the Lord, we cannot sit easily in the seats of wealth and power of an oppressive status quo." (Lifestyle p. 2)

There is, then, a strong emphasis on the *spirit* with which change is to be sought. While they share with other denominations the rejection of allegiance to any earthly system, they focus more directly on seeking acts that can be done in a Christ-like spirit. (Lifestyle p. 7) Consistent with their history as a "peace church," there is also a strong emphasis on non-violent change.

In short, a number of the same elements are present here as in the mainline statements: respect and equality, special emphasis on the poor, refusal to condone any earthly system of economics, attention to systemic problems, notions of stewardship and responsibility, criticism of the "money culture" and acquisitiveness of people. Yet these elements take on a distinctive character as they are cast within the purview of a people who are examining first their own house and their own complicity with injustice, who seek only those actions consistent with a certain "spirit," and who eschew earthly power as central to the task of economic renewal and justice. The witness of the church is primary, and the church is to serve others in the spirit and style of Jesus.[2]

VII. Concluding Remarks

All of the Protestant groups considered here approach economic justice by use of biblical vision and analogy. What we are to do is discerned by looking at what is said or done in scripture. If God covenants with a people, then we are to understand ourselves as being communal by nature, and act accordingly. If Jesus cared for the poor, then we are to have special regard for the poor. If stewardship is an important biblical category, then it remains the model for human action today.

This is not *per se* an ethic of imitation. We are not simply to

---

2. According to Severyn T. Bruyn, the Quakers would also exhibit many of these characteristics. They have often formed alternative communities to be living examples of a different lifestyle, they focus on the importance of sharing power and of "gentleness" in style, and they urge both small and global actions that eschew nationalities and governments. See Bruyn, "Quaker Testimonies and Economic Alternatives," Pendle Hill Pamphlet 231, 1980.

do what Jesus did, or what the ancient Israelites did. (Indeed, there is a striking absence of references, for example, to the parable of the good Samaritan and the command to "go thou and do likewise.") Rather, the argument grounds ethical standards in our identity as Christians. Christian identity is central to determining what one is to do. This identity is given at least in large part by reference to the story of a people long ago and how they understood God to act in their lives, as recorded in scripture. In essence, the Protestant statements assume that if scripture holds that we were created in God's image, this affirmation remains true today and continues to provide insight for ethical behavior.

At root, therefore, the ethic is biblically based ("sola scriptura"). Yet reason is important in determining the proper application of biblical themes to the contemporary situation: "It is not possible or useful to try to pretend that twentieth century America could or should duplicate the political and economic system of Israel." (UPCUSA #073; cf. UCC #48) Economic ethics is not a matter of attempting to reconstruct a biblical world. But it is nonetheless closely linked to the vision of justice given in the biblical worlds of ancient Israel and the early Christian communities as they struggled to discern God's presence and call. Further, it is largely a creation theology, drawing heavily on the creation stories rather than on apocalyptic materials, wisdom literature, or other biblical sources.

The movement is from general theological concepts (e.g. image of God) to ethical mandates (e.g. respect for all persons) and then to the application of those mandates. For the mainline groups, the defining ethical category is *justice* rather than love, charity, compassion, humility, or other possible categories. "Of all the biblical and theological themes that we reviewed in our search for clues as to what faithfulness to God requires of us here and now, none seemed more relevant than the one that witnesses to the justice that God does and expects." (UPCUSA #309)

The place where the mainline groups and the Brethren split is on the emphasis or audience. Mainline Protestants join with the National Conference of Catholic Bishops in wanting to address society at large and to impact social policy primarily. They offer an "ethics of policy." This may also be why they stress justice rather than love, charity, or other more limited Christian concepts as the central ethical category—justice is a term that resonates with the values embodied in American history ("liberty and justice for all") and which therefore seems more general and less sectarian than, for example, the emphasis on service and humility offered by the Church of the Brethren.

A number of issues remain for these groups. First, although all mainline groups stress justice, almost none of them define the concept. Only the LCA offers a definition and lengthy discussion of justice. It also distinguishes justice from love and posits a need for love as well as justice: "Neither personal nor corporate benevolence can accomplish what a society is required to do for its members under justice; but a society cannot remain sound if it leaves no room for benevolent acts." (LCA p. 4) Other groups, however, utilize the concept of justice largely without careful definition. If justice is to be the defining category, then a careful definition of the concept is needed.

Second, dependence on scripture as the base for an economic ethic suggests that attention should be given to hermeneutical issues regarding the interpretation and use of scripture.[3] For example, most Protestant groups depend heavily on Jesus' proclamation as recorded in Luke 4:18, yet they fail to recognize that Luke's gospel overall addresses economic justice from an ameliorating stance rather than calling for radical reform or revolution.

Third, the movement from theological affirmations to norms to application utilizes traditional deductive modes that have difficulty letting experience speak. While considerable attention is given to statistics regarding poverty, and an "option for the poor" emerges as a norm for most groups, the voices of the poor themselves are not readily heard nor sought. At best, major Protestant groups have not yet adopted a thorough option for the poor in which the views of poor people would become definitive both

---

3. I wish to express my gratitude here to Stephen Breck Reid of Pacific School of Religion for his helpful analyses of the uses of scripture by Protestant groups.

for understanding injustices and for proposing correctives. At worst, the poor receive no special attention at all, as is the case in the LCA document.

Further, Camenisch argues rightly that most of the Protestant groups draw back from the radical implications that might be embedded in the scriptural view taken.[4] For example, most do *not* suggest that Christians need to become poor themselves. Camenisch argues that, as important as some aspects of their work may be, "these documents must still be faulted for not putting to the churches challenges commensurate with the seriousness of the problems they portray and the potential radicalness of the biblical foundations they cite."[5] Most of the statements remain well within the basic assumptions of American culture and its capitalist economic system: although they may offer some criticisms of capitalism, most do not propose a switch to a different system. Thus, the solutions proposed are rarely of a radical and far-reaching nature.

Here is where the Church of the Brethren may have something to offer to the mainline groups from its Anabaptist tradition. Its argument is oriented precisely to the question of Christian witness. Where other groups draw back from the implications of their insights for Christian living and tend instead to focus on social policy and governmental responsibility, the Brethren offer concrete suggestions focused directly at their own members' lives.

The difference here between the Church of the Brethren and the mainline Protestant groups takes us directly to a root problem for Protestants. Protestants ground their ethics in a scriptural vision. But this very grounding raises the question of how one is to speak to those outside the faith.

The Brethren answer this question by speaking primarily to those inside. They do not presume that their arguments will be compelling for non-Christians, and they are able to work concretely in terms of biblical requirements. Yet in so doing, they

---

4. Paul F. Camenisch, "Recent Mainline Protestant Statements on Economic Justice," *Annual* of the Society of Christian Ethics, 1987, p. 74.
5. Ibid., p. 72.

lose some ability to impact governmental and social policy outside the purview of the church.

The mainline groups answer the question by assuming that the general norms drawn from the biblical vision will be consonant with societal notions of justice and equality, and therefore that they can appeal to those beyond the faith. They gain political impact. But in so doing, they tend to lose specificity and open themselves to the charge that they have failed to take the potentially radical demands of faith sufficiently seriously.

Both mainline and sectarian Protestant groups have begun to demonstrate serious concern about economic justice. But some fundamental questions remain to be answered.

5. Jewish Statements on Social Justice

David Biale

Both Jewish organizations and individual Jews have been at the forefront of a variety of movements in America for social change and economic justice over the last hundred years. The disproportionate involvement of Jews in these movements is often explained by the argument that the Jewish tradition decries economic inequality and exhorts Jews to fight for a just social order. Yet, in the last decade, neo-conservative voices in the Jewish world have challenged this identification of the Jewish tradition with political liberalism or social democracy. The most recent statements by Jewish religious and communal organizations on issues of economic and social justice do not, however, support the contention that Jews no longer identify with a progressive agenda, but the question of just what role the Jewish tradition plays in shaping the social consciousness of Jews is valid and important. In order to analyze recent Jewish statements on economic and social issues, it is necessary first to examine what the Jewish tradition has to say about these issues and to identify those sources that can prove relevant to a quest for social justice. It will then be possible to draw conclusions about the nature of Jewish statements in relation to the Jewish tradition.

Economic and Social Justice in the Jewish Tradition

The biblical text is exquisitely sensitive to the plight of the poor in society. The book of Deuteronomy states:

> If, however, there is a needy person among you . . . do
> not harden your heart and shut your hand against your

needy kinsman. Rather, you must open your hand and lend him sufficient for whatever he needs. . . . Give to him readily and have no regrets when you do so, for in return the Lord your God will bless you in all your efforts and in all your undertakings. For there will never cease to be needy ones in your land, which is why I command you: open your hand to the poor and needy kinsman in your land (Dt 15:7–8, 10–11).

All those on the margins of society, such as widows, orphans and resident aliens, are treated with special consideration by biblical law. The poor are not only to be cared for by society, but they must not be discriminated against. The law requires equitable and humane treatment of the economically disadvantaged:

> You shall not abuse a needy and destitute laborer, whether a fellow countryman or a stranger in one of the communities of your land. You must pay him his wages on the same day, before the sun sets, for he is needy and urgently depends on it . . . (Dt 24:14–15).

The theological grounding for such treatment of the poor is the egalitarian covenant between the Israelites and God, a covenant that also includes non-Israelite residents of the land. Deuteronomy 29:9–10 specifies that the covenant between God and his people includes not only "your tribal heads, your elders and your officials," but also "your children, your wives, even the stranger within your camp, from woodchopper to waterdrawer."

Repeatedly, the Bible grounds concern for the poor in the experience of the Israelites as slaves in Egypt (Dt 15:15; 24:17, 22). Since selling oneself into slavery was often the only recourse of a poor person in the ancient world, helping the poor was a way of preventing enslavement. Biblical law was equally solicitous of those who became slaves: they were to be treated humanely and, if they were Hebrew slaves, they were to be offered their freedom every seventh year.

Laws pertaining to the poor can be divided into two broad classes which, in turn, reflect two different points of view. The first might be called laws to *ameliorate poverty,* such as the right of the poor to eat from a neighboring vineyard or field (Dt 23:25–26) or the commandment to leave the remainder of the harvest to the poor (Dt 24:19–21). These laws clearly reflect a belief that poverty is an inevitable condition that can only be tempered but not eliminated: "There will never cease to be needy ones in your land, which is why I command you: open your hand to the poor and needy kinsman in your land" (Dt 15:11).

Other laws, however, have a more utopian vision and strive to *make society more egalitarian.* One example is the prohibition of usury (Ex 22:24; Lev 25:36). The laws pertaining to sabbatical remission of debts (Dt 15:1–5) and the jubilee return of lands to their original owners (Lev 25) were also designed to prevent the development of immutable economic classes. As Deuteronomy 15 states: "There shall be no needy among you, since the Lord your God will bless you in the land that the Lord your God is giving you as a hereditary portion."

The theology that underlies the jubilee laws is the radical notion that "the land must not be sold beyond reclaim, for the land is mine; you are but strangers resident with me" (Lev 25:23). God is the ultimate landlord. This theological principle, which has been quoted with enthusiasm by socialists seeking religiously grounded sources, must not, however, be misunderstood in its biblical setting. The intent of the biblical laws was not to undermine the concept of private property altogether, but rather to prevent the alienation of patrimonial lands, a problem that evidently became quite severe during the monarchy.

For all the egalitarian intent behind the sabbatical remission of debts, the law, in fact, could be counterproductive, for the rich often refrained from loaning money to the poor before the sabbatical. In Second Temple times, Hillel (early first century) devised a waiver, called the *prosbul,* that allowed repayment of debts despite the sabbatical.

The prophets were as obsessed with the plight of the poor as were the legal codes. It is likely that early nomadic Israelite society was relatively egalitarian, but social distinctions became increasingly pronounced during the monarchy. The prophetic movement, starting with Amos and Hosea, may have emerged partly as a response to the new social situation of the eighth century. In general, the denunciations of ill-treatment of the poor by prophets such as Amos, Hosea, Isaiah and Jeremiah are not based on a radical critique of the structure of society, but on the systematic failure of the rich to obey the laws requiring solicitude for the poor. Amos denounces the "cows of Bashan on the hill of Samaria who defraud the poor, who rob the needy" (Am 4:1). He attacks their behavior, not the existence of private wealth as such.

If the prophets did not criticize the social system for creating poverty, neither did they hold the poor responsible for their condition. The wisdom literature reflects a different point of view and it does blame the poor for laziness and other qualities (Prov 6:6–11; 13:18). The aristocratic author of a Second Temple work like Ben Sirah not only assumes a hierarchical and unegalitarian society, but he denies the ability of the working classes to play a role in political life.

Similar tensions can be found in rabbinic statements on poverty. Many texts consider poverty endemic and also "the worst of all sufferings in the world" (Exodus Rabba 31:12). The rabbis recognized that poverty also involves humiliation and they prescribe giving charity in ways that will lessen as much as possible the humiliation that the poor feel in receiving assistance. For example, one of the highest forms of charity is to give in such a way that neither the giver nor the recipient is aware of each other's identity.

On the other hand, since giving charity is considered a very important commandment and since fulfilling a commandment brings one a reward, some texts indicate that God intends that there be inequalities in wealth in order to give people the opportunity to fulfill the commandment of giving charity (Tosefta Peah 4:18, BT Baba Batra 10a). The poor are seen, according to this point of view, as a permanent, divinely created feature of society; charity cannot eliminate but only ameliorate poverty.

A major contemporary question is whether systems of social welfare should be directed by principles of charity or of justice. The Jewish tradition has much to say on this issue. The term for the commandment of charity is *zedakah*, which means righteousness and is derived from *zedek*, which means justice. Assistance to the poor is not a discretionary matter; it is obligatory and falls in the realm of justice. As Moses Maimonides, the great twelfth century legal authority and philosopher, wrote: "Gifts to the poor are not benevolence, but debts." Even the poor themselves are required to give *zedakah* from the *zedakah* they receive. A famous story in the Talmud tells of a poor man who told a rabbi that he always ate fatted chickens and drank old wine. The rabbi, astonished at this extravagance, asked him whether he didn't feel that he had made himself a burden on the community. The poor man replied: "Do I eat what is theirs? I eat what is God's" (Ketubot 67b). From a theological point of view, the giving of charity is not only a commandment from God, it is also a form of redistribution of the wealth that is originally God's.

Throughout the centuries, philanthropy was one of the central activities of the Jewish community. Indeed, *zedakah* was for the most part a communal rather than an individual activity. The poor were discouraged from begging from individuals and were, instead, required to register with the community's poor fund. Anyone who settled in a community for more than thirty days was required to contribute to the charity fund. A quasi-governmental structure of welfare mediated between the givers and receivers of charity and thus gave concrete expression to the right of the poor to public assistance. By creating such structures, charity lost many of its humiliating qualities. In addition, Jewish courts could expropriate private property from those who failed to fulfill their charitable obligations. This form of coercive taxation demonstrates that private property rights were not considered absolute. The Jewish tradition therefore is entirely consistent with the modern notion of a welfare state in which governments assume the obligation of assisting the poor, the wealthy are taxed and the poor are considered to be entitled to this assistance.

Although rabbinic Judaism did not believe that poverty could be eliminated, the highest form of charity was to help a poor person support himself, by "a loan, or the forming of a partnership with him for the transaction of some business enterprise, or assistance in obtaining some employment for him, so that he will not be forced to seek charity from his fellow men" (Moses Maimonides, *Mishneh Torah,* "Laws of Gifts to the Poor," 10:7–14).

The tradition regards work as an intrinsic value and the poor were obliged to work rather than simply accept alms. Human dignity therefore required that a poor person be given the means to sustain himself.

The rabbis had no systematic economic theory or vision of how an economy should be structured. Yet, it is clear from rabbinic law that they did not believe in a "free market." They regulated profits and interest rates according to specific formulas; they also had a clear notion of the labor value inherent in any commodity, similar to medieval Christian concepts. In these respects, the rabbis were products of a pre-capitalist economic system.

Despite both the theology and the institutional structures of *zedakah,* in practice, wealth was never redistributed in Jewish communities throughout the middle ages. The wealthy householders governed the communities, and although one of their main communal activities was philanthropy, no attempt was made to eliminate poverty as such or to share political power with the poor.

Despite some theological statements that might be appropriated by an ideology of radical redistribution of property, the Jewish tradition cannot be considered inherently socialist. The egalitarian character of early Israelite society was replaced by a hierarchical society in monarchic times; in the middle ages, the Jews constituted a quasi-capitalist element in feudal society. The commercial and financial activities that provided the Jews with their main sources of income throughout the middle ages virtually guaranteed that wealth would be distributed unequally. Law and tradition sought to control and limit the most glaring inequities of this reality, but they did not prescribe systemic transformations.

Recent Jewish Statements on Economic Justice

The structure of contemporary Jewish life makes it considerably more difficult to define *the* Jewish position on any question today than it was before modern times (even in the ancient and medieval periods, opinions can be found along a broad spectrum on almost every issue). No longer do rabbinical authorities have a monopoly on normative statements and even the rabbinical world is split into a myriad of movements, from Reform to Conservative to a wide variety of Orthodox factions. There are a large number of non-religious Jewish organizations engaged in philanthropic, political and social action that have also taken stands on contemporary issues. As opposed to the Catholic Church and the denominations of Protestantism, the Jewish community is more than a religious body, even a religious body divided into a number of movements. It is also an ethnic community that defines a certain political agenda quite apart from purely religious or spiritual principles. Given this rather anarchic reality, it is hard to imagine a Jewish analog to the pastoral letter on the U.S. economy by the National Conference of Catholic Bishops, a statement with the full pedagogical authority of the sole official spokesmen for American Catholicism.

The Jewish organizations that have issued statements on economic issues represent only certain fractions of the American Jewish community. The closest parallel to the bishops' letter or to the position statements of some of the Protestant denominations are the statements by the Union of American Hebrew Congregations, the umbrella organization of Reform Judaism (actually, the Central Conference of American Reform Rabbis would be more like the National Conference of Catholic Bishops, but no statement on economic justice is available from that body). The other statements before us stem from the American Jewish Congress, the American Jewish Committee and the National Jewish Community Relations Advisory Council. The first two are non-religious Jewish political organizations. The last is an umbrella organization for a myriad of religious and non-religious groups: its position reflects a kind of consensus of American Jewish organizations, but because it represents such a diverse constituency, it is rarely able to articulate a clear vision of social alternatives.

With this introduction, it is possible to say a few things about the common characteristics of all these statements. From a political point of view, they all tend to criticize aspects of the Reagan administration's budget and social policy. They put the highest priority on a national social agenda that meets human needs and works toward equality. They oppose dismantling social programs in favor of disproportionate military expenditures. In general, they favor the welfare state that was created over the last half century and seek to fulfill its vision of full employment and elimination of poverty. To be sure, there are nuances of differences between different groups, with the liberal American Jewish Congress taking perhaps the most outspoken position. But the statements reflect a virtual consensus that grows out of the still overwhelming tendency of American Jews to vote for the Democratic Party. To this extent, the arguments of the Jewish neo-conservatives have made little dent on the Jewish organizations represented here.

Yet, there are several aspects of these statements that deserve critical comment. First, there is something striking about those groups that are *not* represented. Neither the Conservative nor the Orthodox movement has developed comprehensive statements on economic justice. With the exception of the statements of the Reform Movement, the religious leaders of the Jewish community as collective bodies have been strangely silent at a time when Catholic and Protestant authorities have been taking an increasingly active role in public debate.

Second, the statements by and large do not ground their political recommendations in the Jewish tradition. Occasional passing references to the Bible, and, in one instance, to Moses Maimonides, can be found in the Reform statements. In one place, to be sure, the UAHC argues that "Judaism teaches that no economic system is sacred; human beings and human needs are sacred. Any economic system deserves to survive only if it effectively provides for the well-being of the least powerful, least advantaged members of society." This strong position is not given any kind of systematic treatment in terms of Jewish sources. No attempt is made to ask what kind of economic system might satisfy the criteria of Jewish tradition.

Yet, as perfunctory as the Reform statements are in their theological grounding, the non-religious organizations do not even go this far. Taken as a whole, the theological weakness of these statements is strikingly at odds with the way the Christian statements, especially those of the American and Canadian bishops, appeal extensively and systematically to traditional principles. The intent of the Catholic statements in particular is to challenge current American values with an avowedly alternative world-view.

Finally, the statements concern themselves almost exclusively with specific issues such as unemployment, wage discrimination, health care and homelessness. They do not put these issues in any larger context or develop any systematic analysis of the nature of the modern economy as do, for example, the Canadian bishops. Neither do we find here any vision of alternatives, except for support for the conventional nostrums of the mainline Democratic Party. The kind of bold challenge rooted in a theological critique of the modern economy to be found in the Canadian bishops' statement or, to a somewhat lesser degree, in the pastoral letter of the American bishops is conspicuously absent in the Jewish statements. Surely our brief summary of the Jewish tradition suggests that a rich treasury of values can be identified in Jewish sources which might be brought to bear on an analysis of the problems of the modern American economy.

An Analysis of the Jewish Statements

The failings of the Jewish statements, especially in contrast to the very interesting developments in the Christian churches, are especially striking given the deserved reputation of Jews for activism in struggles for economic and social justice. Why this reticence at a time when other religions are speaking out so forcefully?

Several tentative answers can be given. First, it may be a mistake to connect the Jewish social activism of the last hundred years with the teachings of the tradition. Although Jewish liberals and socialists often appropriated specific statements from the tradition, usually from the prophetic and deuteronomic texts of the Bible, the real impetus for their activity did not come from spiritual sources. Indeed, religious figures, with a few notable exceptions, played only minor roles in the political, economic and social movements in Europe and America in which Jews took part. This observation is especially true for the Orthodox, who would have been more likely than others to draw their inspiration from the tradition.

Jewish social activism owes its vitality to the tortuous process of emancipation in Europe. The emergence of a secularized group of Jews in countries such as Germany, Austro-Hungary and Russia at the end of the nineteenth century, where Jewish emancipation was either incomplete or entirely thwarted, created social ferment. Unable to achieve full integration in the societies in which they lived but unwilling to return to medieval patterns of living, they turned to radical ideas for social change. If society would not free them, they would transform society.

As anti-semitism increased and became more violent toward the end of the nineteenth century, Jews sought either revolutionary solutions or left Europe entirely. Those who came to America in the great waves of immigration between 1881 and 1924 brought with them these new radical ideas. The immigrants frequently broke away from traditional Judaism in the process of migration. Since few rabbis accompanied these immigrants, the American Jewish community that emerged was less steeped in traditional sources and less responsive to traditional authorities. It might be said that the new movements for social change, including liberalism and socialism, were all secular substitutes for earlier religious systems of belief.

Many of those Jews who threw themselves into social activism in the twentieth century did so in conscious repudiation of the Orthodox Jewish tradition. An echo of this hostility to Orthodoxy can be found in a statement by the American Jewish Congress entitled "The Jewish Rationale for Social America." The statement argues that:

> The isolation and persecution of Jewry until the Age of Enlightenment and Jewish emancipation necessitated the almost complete concentration of Jewish spirit and intellect on the practice and study of ritual. Halakhah (ritual) was a protective fence not only around the Torah but around the whole of Judaism and Jewry. As a result, the image of Judaism has become one largely of prayer, ritual and study. Although these are undoubtedly

major aspects of Judaism, without which Judaism would
not survive, they are not the complete picture. Deuteronomy and the Prophets are not less essential parts of
our ancient tradition than Leviticus and the Shulkhan
Arukh. The resolutions adopted by the AJCongress . . .
manifest a deep concern for peace, justice, freedom and
equality, and such a concern is as much a moral imperative of historic Judaism as is the concern for ritual and
prayer.

This statement reflects an extraordinarily narrow understanding
of rabbinic law (*halakhah*). As we have seen above, the rabbinic
sources expand and continue the principles of social justice
found in the Bible and, in fact, they form a much richer basis for
social action than does the Bible by itself. But the tendency, also
pronounced in many statements of the Reform movement, to
proceed as if the Jewish tradition since biblical times has little to
say on matters of social concern, gives many contemporary Jewish
statements on justice their curiously "non-Jewish" character.
While this generalization does not apply to arguments for economic and social transformation by individual Jews, some of
whom have grounded their claims in Jewish sources, it does appear to be true of the organizational statements considered here.
     Certainly, such would not be true if the more traditional
movements were to make systematic statements on economic
justice. However, Orthodox Judaism has been conservative on
social issues since emancipation; the Orthodox have often identified with conservative forces in society as the best protectors of
the rights of all religious people. Consequently, they have a more
conservative voting record than more religiously liberal Jews.
Although the sources from the Orthodox (i.e. rabbinic) tradition
provide excellent support for contemporary policies of social
welfare and governmental intervention in the economy, many
Orthodox Jews have articulated much more conservative positions, a result more of a contemporary Orthodox mentality than of
the teachings of their own tradition.
     The Jewish community in America has undergone a dramatic
and virtually unprecedented transformation in the last hundred

years. The artisans and petty merchants who came to America became part of the industrial proletariat. But within one or two generations, their descendants had risen into the commercial and professional middle class in such overwhelming numbers that the generation of the grandsons and granddaughters bears virtually no resemblance to that of its grandparents. If an earlier generation was fighting for political, economic and social rights for itself, the last thirty years or more have seen Jews fighting essentially for the rights of others. Although the vast majority of Jews remain committed to the general principles of economic equality and social justice for which their grandparents and parents struggled, there is perhaps a growing sense that Jews need no longer help themselves by helping others. In other words, the earlier argument held that the tenuous position of Jews in America would be strengthened if the society as a whole became more egalitarian: the Jewish history of persecution made the Jews more sensitive to the persecution and degradation of others and more aware that the fate of the Jews depended on the nature of society as a whole. Now that Jews have "made it" and anti-semitism is no longer a widespread roadblock to social advancement, this argument has begun to lose its force. Perhaps it is less necessary for many to frame American social questions in terms of either Jewish self-interest or the teachings of the Jewish tradition.

The increasing preoccupation with defense of Israel in the last twenty years has possibly also played a role in the lack of recent systematic thinking on social policy. American Jews became much more concerned about Israel with the Six Day War of 1967, at exactly the time that the civil rights movement, in which they had played such a major role, turned toward black nationalism. In the subsequent twenty years, the political activity of Jewish organizations became more and more focused around defense of Israel. Indeed, international concerns take up the first part of the National Jewish Community Relations Advisory Council booklet from 1986–87. The chapter on social and economic justice comes last.

Finally, the failure to make a bold claim on the American public imagination in terms of Jewish tradition, as do the Catholic bishops in terms of Catholic teaching, may have much to do with persistent sensitivity by Jews to being a minority in a Christian country. Although Jews generally do not feel themselves to be the targets of discrimination, many are still reluctant to take part in national domestic debates as Jews rooted in Jewish tradition. In particular, those Jews with progressive social views, such as Reform Jews, are often the most fearful of mixing church and state by introducing "religious" arguments into political discourse. All of the general statements considered here contain strong affirmations of the importance of total separation of church and state in American political life, a position not advanced with quite the same ideological fervor by Orthodox Jews.

On this score there is quite a discrepancy between the Jewish and especially the Catholic point of view. While the bishops are careful to say that theirs is not doctrinal teaching, they do believe that their religious tradition has something important to contribute to the debate on a host of issues in American political life. They wish not only to guide Catholics but also to introduce different values into the general political debate. The historical involvement of the Church in the affairs of the world serves as the precedent for this willingness to take a stand on contemporary issues.

Jewish organizations consider the church-state issue to be so crucial that they often bend over backward to avoid introducing traditional values or language into political discourse (an exception to this generalization would be the statements by American Jewish Committee Task Forces on poverty, the elderly and the family; all of these statements include chapters on Jewish teachings in the belief that the tradition can enrich the general public debate on these issues). Here, then, are two very different visions of the role of religious traditions in the political life of a secular society, two different visions of what the separation of church and state might mean.

Jews have historically seen America, for all its imperfections, as a *goldene medina,* a "golden country," far superior to almost all of the other countries in which they have lived over the millennia. They not only have identified totally with American values but often also believe that Judaism is identical to the American ethos. This stance makes it difficult for many Jews to challenge

American society on the basis of their own tradition. Those who wish to offer a radical criticism often feel unconsciously compelled to do so from a position outside the tradition. The Catholic bishops take a very different position. Their belief that the Catholic tradition offers an alternative world-view to some fundamental American values reflects a greater willingness to fight for systemic change.

Yet, it is possible that as Jews feel more and more secure in their position in America, they will be more willing to prod their religious and political institutions to return to the tradition for sources for social change and economic justice. Perhaps the very challenge of the Christian statements on economic justice may provide the catalyst for this much-needed development.

PART III

RESPONDING TO THE STATEMENTS:
A VARIETY OF CRITIQUES

6. Economic Justice and Corporate America

John Oliver Wilson

Over a half century ago, a well-known British economist set the tone for the current discussion on economic justice and corporate America. Lord Lionel Robbins wrote an influential essay on the nature and significance of economic science in which he stated: "Economics deals with ascertainable facts; ethics with valuations and obligations. The two fields of enquiry are not on the same plane of discourse."

This view well characterizes much of American political and religious thinking, along with that of corporate America. Corporations are a creation of the state established to perform the function of efficiently transforming certain inputs of labor, capital, technology and natural resources into consumable commodities. If, in the process of achieving efficiency, the economic system generates a distribution of income that is deemed by society as socially undesirable, it is the responsibility of government to achieve distributive justice through a system of taxes and government expenditures.

This view worked well for many years as the American economy enjoyed an unprecedented period of economic growth and economic isolation. During the post-war period, the years dating from the end of World War II to 1973, the American economy dominated the world economy and enjoyed such strong economic growth that there seemed to be ample opportunities for nearly all Americans to participate in the economic system. It was easy to achieve sufficient distributive justice to satisfy the majority of Americans, produce a surplus to redistribute economic necessities through government programs and private philanthropy to those who were excluded from the system, and to mask some of the more subtle forms of economic injustice that permeated our economic institutions.

That era is now gone. America no longer enjoys the dominance it once did in the global economy. Economic surpluses for redistribution are far harder to come by in an economy that is growing more slowly and confronts increasing needs of the elderly, minority groups, children and women. And the ravages of increased competition from abroad, rapid technology change, corporate takeovers, and massive restructuring of corporations have left many who once felt secure in corporate America with a strong sense that economic injustices are rampant throughout the system and impact all Americans.

Given such an environment, it is little wonder that the statements on economic justice by our major church denominations have recently appeared. There is no more pressing issue that confronts the American economy today than restoring a feeling of security and legitimacy to our economic system, and the church statements force us to confront that reality—Lionel Robbins to the contrary. However, in joining the debate between economics and ethics, the church statements lead us far beyond the intellectual confines in which such debates have taken place in the past. The statements force us to confront two quite different views of our economic system.

The *first* view is the more traditional, and poses the problem in terms that most Americans can readily understand. It is a view that economic justice involves a system that favors certain groups of Americans and excludes others, a system in which confrontation between the "haves" and the "have nots" is inescapable, a system in which government must take the dominant role in achieving greater economic justice, and an economic system that essentially functions much the same as conventionally assumed by economists and government policy-makers. This view is well expressed in the Protestant church statements.

The *second* view is quite different. The conventional model of economic efficiency that guides the behavior of individual consumers, corporate managers, and government policy-makers, the accepted approaches to resolving conflicts between operating an efficient economy and achieving an equitable distribution of income and wealth, and even the basic premises upon which our economic institutions have been founded are challenged by the Catholic statement. That statement speaks of concepts that are foreign and alien to nearly everything that we traditionally think of as characterizing the American economic system.

In essence, the church statements on economic justice raise three significant issues regarding our understanding of our present economic system. First, what is the meaning of economic justice? Second, what is our conceptualization of the economic system through which justice is to be achieved? Third, through what means can we achieve a more just economic system?

1. The Meaning of Economic Justice

The standard dictionary definition of justice refers to the quality of being right or correct, and the attainment of fairness or impartiality. *The Encyclopedia of Philosophy* distinguishes between two different meanings of justice: corrective or *retributive* justice and *distributive* justice. The former concerns lawfulness and the means by which a society determines correct or lawful behavior and appropriate punishments for wrongdoing. The latter concerns the problems of allocating the benefits available in a society among individuals and groups, and arises because of the limitations of human benevolence and the competition for scarce goods.

The definitions of justice that are prevalent in the various church statements incorporate all of these traditional meanings, and then expand the concept of justice with a biblically based understanding. Yet a careful reading of the definition of justice in the Protestant statements and that of the Catholic Church reveal quite different concepts of what is meant by justice.* These dif-

---

* In this paper, I draw primarily upon two of the statements: "Toward a Just, Caring and Dynamic Political Economy," Presbyterian Church (U.S.A.), and *Economic Justice for All,* National Conference of Catholic Bishops. These two statements represent the most thorough and substantive analysis of the issue, and they state most clearly the different concepts of economic justice that are prevalent in our secular as well as our religious discussions today. Throughout this paper specific references and quotes are from these two documents.

ferences are extremely important, for they provide the first indication that the Protestant statements and the Catholic statement view the problem of achieving economic justice in our society in quite different terms. But these differences go far beyond that of simply a Protestant versus a Catholic view of the issue; they go to the heart of the matter of achieving a more just economic system.

The Protestant statements speak of three kinds of justice: retributive justice, distributive justice, and productive justice. *Retributive justice* is quite similar to that of the philosophers as noted above, and concerns issues of lawful behavior and just punishment for wrongdoing. But the Protestant statements add an important element drawn from biblical teachings: retributive justice originates from our relationship to God. We "are sinners in the sight of the creator God . . . we find the corruption of sin in our lives and everywhere in our world . . . we are sinful creatures standing under God's judgment . . . we are to seek justice in the world because that quest reflects the character of the God who is simultaneously righteous and just."

This view has three significant implications: first, it segregates the just from the unjust; second, it establishes a clear hierarchy in the relationship of the just with the unjust; third, it places the entire debate within the context of a confrontation between the just and the unjust. These concepts of segregation, hierarchy, and confrontation dominate all aspects of the Protestant statements, including the remaining two definitions of justice.

Distributive justice requires equal respect and concern for all, special concern for the poor and the oppressed, and response to basic human needs for all. The economic system is to be judged according to what it does "for the poorest, the richest, and those in between (and) movement from injustice toward justice always exacts a price, especially from those who have benefited from injustice."

Productive justice is concerned with how individuals are able to participate in the production process of an economic system, that is, including all members of a society in economic opportunities and economic decisions. "We need to be particularly aware of the ways in which the poor and minorities—racial, ethnic and sexual—may be systematically excluded from economic opportunities and productive decisions and activities.''

The Catholic meaning of economic justice incorporates many of the same elements as do the Protestant statements, but the general context in which these elements are stated gives the overall meaning of economic justice of the Catholics a significantly different sense. For the Catholics, economic justice consists of commutative justice, distributive justice, and social justice.

Commutative justice calls for fundamental fairness in all agreements and exchanges between individuals or private social groups. ''It demands respect for the equal human dignity of all persons in economic transactions, contracts, or promises.''

Distributive justice requires that the allocation of income, wealth, and power in society be evaluated in light of its effects on persons whose basic material needs are unmet. ''If individuals are to be recognized as members of the human community, then the community has an obligation to help fulfill these basic needs unless an absolute scarcity of resources makes this strictly impossible.''

Social justice implies that persons have an obligation to be active and productive participants in the life of society and that society has a duty to enable them to participate in this way. Economic production must be assessed in light of its ''impact on the fulfillment of basic needs, employment levels, patterns of discrimination, environmental quality, and sense of community.''

As opposed to the Protestant meaning of justice, which imbues a strong sense of segregation, hierarchy, and conflict as expressed in the statements quoted above, the Catholic meaning of justice imbues a strong sense of inclusivity—all individuals and groups in society are included in the definition and quoted statements. Indeed, the Catholic definitions can be appropriately characterized by the concepts of interdependency, cooperation, and community.

2. The Conceptualization of the Economic System

The conceptualization of the economic system refers to the particular model which underlies the various Church statements. Understanding such a model is important, for it determines how a particular church statement perceives that economic justice is to be attained within a given economic system. Again, we find significant differences between the model implicit within the Protestant statements and the model implicit in the Catholic statement. The Protestant model is one of a hierarchical relationship between the major actors in an economic system: the individual, the family, the community, the corporation, and government. The Catholic model is one of an interdependent communal relationship between these same actors. Both models are shown graphically below.

The Protestant model begins with the individual who forms the basis of the economic system. Each individual matters, for he or she is created in the image of God. Thus each individual has inherent value and worth independent of nationality, race, social status, income level, family background, educational level or occupation. The economic system exists to encourage and protect individual initiative, and to ensure that each individual has equal access to the opportunity to realize his or her economic potential. And for those whose potential is inadequate to attain sufficient economic means to support a minimal lifestyle, the just economic system must take actions to redistribute income and wealth to provide each individual the basic needs of food, clothing, health care and shelter.

Next in the hierarchy is the family. The family "is the social base on which a society builds its stability, nurtures its young, and helps them assimilate the values that will guide their choices as adults." While these functions must increasingly be carried out in new, different and extended families, as compared to the traditional nuclear family structure, the same responsibilities are applicable to both. Whatever the family structure, the family as a social and economic entity constitutes "a caring unit where mutual, voluntary responsibility for its members is accepted and fulfilled."

From the family, we move upward to the community. In

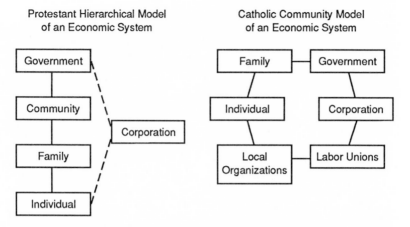

Protestant Hierarchical Model of an Economic System

Catholic Community Model of an Economic System

many respects, the community is viewed as an extended family. We are "born into community, shaped and nurtured in community," much the same as we are born into a family and are shaped and nurtured by that family. "A healthy, prosperous and decent community is what we need and want for ourselves and our children," the same as we want for our family. Furthermore, the community is a covenant community where "we are blessed with forgiveness, and experience wholeness and hope in communion with God and each other," similar to the forgiveness and sense of wholeness that we expect within the family structure. Such a view of community seems to be applicable to a small isolated town. And having grown up in such a town, midwestern and Protestant to its very roots, I can identify with this view of community. But having lived most of my adult life in a large metropolis, I question whether this view of community is applicable to our current age.

Finally, the Protestant model culminates with government. Government is responsible for providing for our social economic needs. These needs include ensuring the security of ourselves and our property, providing for our mutual defense as a national entity, and supplying education, highways, health care and other goods which embody social as well as private benefits. Such a role of government is standard fare for a professional economist. But the Protestant role of government goes far beyond such standard fare. I was amazed to learn that "the Reformed faith has held a very high view of government asserting that its authority and purpose derive from God" and that "Government is God's providential provision for ordering and managing the affairs of society."

Left out of a direct consideration in this hierarchy is the corporation, that entity whose primary responsibility is the production and distribution of the bulk of our economic goods. This seems a rather interesting oversight, particularly since eighty-five percent of all Americans work for private institutions. I would suggest that this omission is far from an oversight, but rather reflects an inherent and dominant characteristic of the Protestant view of economic society.

The corporation is viewed as a necessary evil, maybe a creation of the devil as opposed to government which is the creation of God. The corporation has few merits other than its ability to efficiently transform inputs of labor, capital and resources into desirable economic outputs. It is an entity that must be regulated by government, coerced into behaving in a just and humane fashion by the church, and forever held in low esteem and regarded with suspicion by society. The fact that American corporations are made up of the same individuals who constitute the family, community, government and the church is seemingly overlooked. Nor is it made clear that the same threats to our individual well-being and realization of economic justice inherent in the concentration of power among those who own and manage our corporations is just as true of those who control and manage our government, our universities, and our churches.

In sum, the conceptualization of our economic system as that of a hierarchical relationship between the individual, the family, community, government and the corporation creates an environment in which the achievement of economic justice occurs within the context of conflict between various institutions within our society. Such a conceptualization reinforces the sense of competition and conflict that characterizes the Protestant meaning of economic justice; in particular it sets up economic efficiency in direct conflict with economic justice. Economic justice is seen as more sacred than economic efficiency, and those engaged in the pursuit of economic justice (government and the church) are viewed as operating with a higher set of values than those engaged in the efficient production and distribution of economic goods and services (corporations).

Furthermore, there is a strong sense of retributive justice involved in the process of conflict resolution. Corporation America not only should alter its ways, but it should do penance for its misbehavior. It is no wonder that in such an environment corporations generally consider economic justice as an issue of philanthropy (to be dealt with through corporate contributions to social causes), treating it with benign neglect or passive compliance with perceived social norms (taking the view that government and the church have little knowledge and no experience in the real world of economics), or with outright confrontation (rarely taken for this creates conflict within the individual value systems of corporate managers).

The Catholic model of our economic system is composed of the same major actors as the Protestant model—the individual, the family, the community, the corporation, and government. But the conceptualization of their role and relationship within our society is significantly different. All of the actors are viewed as belonging to a broadly conceived social community—a community characterized by interdependency and cooperation. This community extends far beyond our own national boundaries, for we "are linked in a complex commercial, financial, technological, and environmental network" that is global. Accepting the reality of this global interdependency as the starting point in understanding our American economic system focuses the Catholic statement on the means of achieving "dignity, solidarity, and justice" among all people.

The means for achieving these goals "will call for new forms of cooperation and partnership among those whose daily work is the source of the prosperity and justice of the nation." These new forms must go far beyond the traditional competitive models of institutional and individual behavior that has dominated much of American economic thought and is prevalent throughout the Protestant statements. "Today a greater spirit of partnership and teamwork is needed; competition alone will not do the job. It has too many negative consequences for family life, the economically vulnerable, and the environment."

Given this overall view of a broad social community, the Catholic statement assesses the role of the individual and the family much the same as do the Protestant statements. The individual is created in God's image: "As such every human being possesses an inalienable dignity that stamps human existence prior to any division into races or nations and prior to human labor and human achievement." The family is "the basic building block of any society" and economic arrangements "must support the family and promote its solidity."

However, the achievement of human dignity and the promotion of family solidity is achieved through an interaction with other institutions within our economic system, in particular with corporations, labor unions, local organizations, and government. It is at this point that the Catholic conceptualization of our economic system begins to break with the Protestant model.

For corporations, "new patterns of partnership among those working in individual firms and industries" and those who own and manage those firms must be created. Each individual, whether a worker, manager or shareholder, "makes a contribution to the enterprise, and each has a stake in its growth or decline." But present structures of accountability do not acknowledge all these contributions or protect these stakes. A major challenge "is the development of new institutional mechanisms for accountability that also preserve the flexibility needed to respond quickly to a rapidly changing business environment."

The purpose of labor unions "is not simply to defend the existing wages and prerogatives of the fraction of workers who belong to them, but also to enable workers to make positive and creative contributions to the firm, the community, and the larger society in an organized and cooperative way." At the local level, such units as families, neighborhoods, church congregations, community organizations, civic and business associations, and public interest and advocacy groups must "play a crucial role in generating creative partnerships for the pursuit of the public good." And the challenge for government "is to move beyond abstract disputes about whether more or less government intervention is needed, to consideration of creative ways of enabling government and private groups to work together effectively.''

In sum, the Catholic model views an economic system as composed of interdependent institutions bound together by economic and social interrelationships. None of these institutions stands independent of the others, nor does any single institution enjoy a hierarchical superiority over other institutions in either a perceived role in the economic system or in a conceptualized ability to promote greater economic justice. The achievement of a more just economic system requires the involvement of all institutions.

The basic difference between the achievement of economic justice in the Protestant model and the Catholic model is that the former attempts to achieve justice through a redistribution of economic output *after the fact of the production of that output* (the major reason corporations are excluded from the analysis) while the latter views the achievement of justice as *an integral part of the process of participation in the economic system itself* (the major reason for the overall inclusiveness of the Catholic model).

3. Achieving Economic Justice

Unfortunately, all of the statements are weakest when it comes to creative proposals for achieving greater justice in our economic system. The Protestant proposals are the least disappointing, for they readily follow from the understanding of justice and the conceptualization of our economic system that the Protestants embrace. The means of achieving economic justice represent conventional wisdom and offer nothing new. Greater economic justice is to be achieved through reducing the size of the federal budget deficit, adopting ''a radically simplified tax system,'' reducing military spending, achieving a full-employment economy, implementing a ''notification procedure'' for all institutions that intend to release a sizable number of employees, and reducing world hunger. All of these proposals are standard fare among those who debate the future course of American economic policies, and there are few who would argue that they are not desirable objectives given the current status of our economy. The essential question is: How will achieving all of these objectives increase economic justice? When we search the Protestant statements for answers we find the expected: redistribute the output of our economy, primarily through progressive taxes on income and wealth and increased government spending on programs designed to aid the poor and the unemployed. Achieving distributive justice is certainly important, but economic justice is a far more complex problem than simply redistributing the output of the economy.

The Catholic meaning of justice and conceptualization of our economic system recognizes this complexity, but the Catholic means for achieving justice are nearly identical with those of the Protestants. The Catholic statement offers us a platter full of well-intentioned objectives: Full employment—"the most urgent priority for domestic economic policy is the creation of new jobs with adequate pay and decent working conditions." Poverty —"dealing with poverty is a moral imperative of the highest priority." Food—"food, water, and energy are essential to life." International economics—we must "eliminate the scandal of the shocking inequality between the rich and the poor in a world divided ever more sharply between them."

Furthermore, the solutions for dealing with these problems also are similar to those of the Protestants—increased job-training and apprenticeship programs, the creation of jobs for the long-term unemployed and those with special needs, increased education for the poor, welfare programs that provide recipients with adequate levels of support, redistribution of farm support programs from the large and rich farmers to the small and medium-sized family farmers, and greater financial aid for the third world countries.

Again, we cannot argue against these suggestions, for distributive justice is a significant part of economic justice. But what happened to commutative justice and social justice? Where did the visionary concepts of interdependency, cooperation, and community disappear to in developing means to achieve greater economic justice? Why does the Catholic statement not offer us imaginative *means* to go along with its "call for an imaginative vision of the future that can help shape economic arrangements in creative new ways" to achieve economic justice? The great disappointment of the Catholic statement is that we were offered so much in terms of a new vision of economic justice, and received so little as means for achieving such justice.

While the church statements on economic justice may not have lived up to our expectations, they are very important in what they do accomplish. At a time when American society is searching for its moral foundations, the statements force us to confront the most essential issue regarding the achievement of justice in our economic system: Will greater economic justice be achieved through the traditional means of conflict resolution and redistribution of economic output as suggested by the Protestant statements, or will greater economic justice require that we redefine our economic system and rebuild economic institutions into a true interdependent and cooperative economic community as the Catholic statement suggests?

7. A Response from Working People

Jim Ryder

It is a safe assumption that the majority of the readers of this volume are not members of labor unions, and that many of them harbor the kinds of suspicions of unions that are common throughout the population at large. In recent times, especially during the years of the Reagan administration, labor has been receiving a bad press. Some of this results from charges of corruption within union management, although it should be noted that corruption has been even more widespread among investment consultants who have been exposed for their extensive manipulations of the stock market for personal gain. Most of it, however, is the result of a certain perception of the American economy, based on the assumption that "management" is that part of our society dedicated to a fair shake for all, and that "labor" is a "special interest group" concerned only for its own members, and caring little or nothing for the rest of society.

Without attempting a full-scale rebuttal of this perception —which naturally causes pain to those of us committed to seeing that working people are decently treated and fairly paid— enough should be said to clarify the role of labor in our economy and make possible a fair hearing for the comments made in this chapter.

We can start with an assumption, which I believe the later pages of this essay will corroborate, that the objectives of labor unions are directly parallel to the ethical and moral responsibilities highlighted in the documents of the various religious groups.

Labor unions are unique in our society by virtue of having evolved through the struggle of working people themselves to gain political and economic control over their lives, rather than having such decisions imposed on them by others, as they were for many centuries. Unions are thus in the vanguard of an extensive social revolution that is far from over, in which similar demands for control over their own lives are now being expressed by racial minorities, women, the disabled, gays and lesbians, and —on the global scene—impoverished third world nations. While all these groups are viewed with apprehension by the small minority with most of the power, it should be clear that they are articulating and bringing to fruition the long-deferred dreams and aspirations of the great majority of the human family.

Contrary to much adverse public opinion, unions play a crucial and largely beneficial role in this struggle, seeking to improve the workplace, increase productivity, and reduce inequality. When these goals are not being met, the reason may be that the union does not yet have sufficient power, or that unorganized workers are fearful of joining a union in the face of anticipated management reprisals. A reason often given for occasional union ineffectiveness, e.g. "corruption," not only is an instance of seeking to throw the baby out with the bath water, but wrongly discounts the ability of unions to reform from within on such occasions as is necessary.

Unions provide workers with a measure of job security, fair wages, and benefits (such as vacation pay, health insurance, pensions, etc.) that simply could not be achieved by individuals bargaining on their own. The statistics are clear that not only do union shop workers command higher wages and benefits than their non-union counterparts, but that union activities promote acts of legislation—such as safer working conditions and elimination of racism and sexism in the workplace—that are significant for all workers whether unionized or not, and thus for society as a whole.

It is frequently charged that unions have an unfavorable impact on productivity, but studies by Freeman and Medoff (*What Do Unions Do?* Basic Books, Inc., N.Y. 1984) suggest that "In many sectors, unionized establishments are much more productive than non-union establishments, while in only a few are they less productive. The higher productivity is due in part to a lower rate of turnover under unionism, improved managerial performance and cooperative labor-management relations" (pp. 21–22).

Structurally and organizationally, unions are open, but participation has been on a serious decline for more than two decades. It is a fundamental tenet of democracy that to function well there must be participation of an informed electorate. The shortcomings of most unions are linked to the failure of unions to attract the necessary number of informed participants. Responsibility for this, however, is not to be laid solely at the door of unions and their leadership. The phenomenon is a reflection of societal indifference at large, from voter registration and turnout, to participation of parents in schools and attendance at religious services. Informed participation, not apathy, will provide for a resurgence of democracy that will also propel union organization in the future.

We are forced to add that the Reagan years have been devastating for unions. Since Mr. Reagan broke the PATCO union of air traffic controllers early in his presidency, the message has been clear that the administration is pro-business and anti-labor. The Reagan-appointed National Labor Relations Board (NLRB) has created the largest backlog of cases in the history of the Board. Reagan appointees to the NLRB, charged with protecting workers' rights, have been corporate labor attorneys, members of "union-busting" law firms and Right to Work committees. Established labor law has been reversed and major case law has been recalled, much like the recent decision of the U.S. Supreme Court to review a major civil rights decision.

The trend of mergers and leveraged buyouts, plus the "golden parachute" retirement plans for CEO's, have similarly affected the power of labor to bargain effectively. The fact that over thirty-three million people live below the poverty line (a fact that the Catholic bishops rightly deplore in their pastoral letter) and the administration's steadfast refusal to acknowledge that there is real hunger in the nation only add signs of trouble for members of the working class.

In summary, labor unions provide workers with higher wages, higher fringe benefits, and greater fairness as a result of a voice in the defense of wages, hours and working conditions (grievance/arbitration), and these benefits cut across age, race, and sexual lines as well as blue-collar/white collar distinctions. The data do not support allegations of widespread union corruption, and, in fact, demonstrate far greater corruption in the business world.

Areas of Overlap Between the Concerns of Religion and Labor

In light of the ingrained suspicion of many members of the religious community about the role of labor in general and unions in particular, it may come as an initial surprise to discover how many areas of common concern there actually are between religion and labor.

As far back as 1891, Roman Catholic statements were affirming the rights of labor, and even though such early statements were cautious about the role assigned to unions, the support of the right of workers to organize, bargain collectively, strike, and otherwise demand fairer working conditions has become clearer in each successive document since that time. Similar concern for working people was apparent in statements by the Federal Council of Churches in the United States long before the depression of 1929, and commitments to the rights of workers have continued in the documents of its successor, the National Council of Churches of Christ in America.

In recent times, and in the statements analyzed in this volume, consistent attention is devoted to a "preferential option for the poor," even when that relatively recent phrase is lacking. All the religious bodies recognize that every person has a right to human dignity, a right that can be achieved only in community and through the doing of worthwhile work, and it is virtually axiomatic that working people have the right to form labor unions. In the eyes of the religious communities, therefore, as well as in the unions themselves, labor has great dignity, and these commonalities alone have brought significant alliances for mutual benefit into being.

The *right* to work and the *dignity* of work have become cornerstones of contemporary religious thought. The point is strongly made in Pope John Paul II's recent encyclical, *Laborem Exercens:* "Work is a good thing for persons—a good thing for humanity—because through work persons not only transform nature, adapting it to their own needs, but they also achieve fulfillment as human beings and indeed in a sense become 'more fully human' " (par. 9). The Roman Catholic bishops' pastoral letter on "Economic Justice for All" elaborates the theme: "It is in their daily work, however, that persons become the subjects and creators of the economic life of the nation." Interestingly enough, Karl Marx likewise saw labor as the embodiment of human value, providing a social basis for self-realization while simultaneously providing for material needs, and it is a sign of increasing maturity that church groups can affirm some of the insights propounded by one who for so long they would only castigate. Indeed, as we are seeing more and more clearly, human labor, in conjunction with the development of natural resources, provides the foundation of all economic systems. The Roman Catholic bishops' letter, along with statements by most of the other religious bodies, lays down as a bottom line that people have a *right to employment,* and that in return for their labor, workers have a *right to wages and benefits* that are sufficient to sustain their lives in dignity. Naturally, these are convictions with which those in the labor force and in unions voice agreement, and for which they are constantly working, not simply for their own private benefit but because such provisions are necessary for the smooth working of the economy and thus for the public benefit as well.

The bishops' letter, for example, states that "property owners, managers and investors of financial capital must all contribute to creating a more just society." The emphasis in such statements is *accountability,* not simply the furthering of private interests, and the statement of the Canadian Conference of Catholic Bishops makes the point even more explicitly: "Capital and technology are understood to be the means or instruments of production (and) should be used for humanly constructive purposes."

Central to such concern for the ends for which society is organized is a consistent and deep-running theme that *labor takes precedence over technology and capital*—a theme explicit not only in the various Catholic statements, but in the Presbyterian, Baptist, Quaker, Episcopalian and Disciples of Christ statements as well. The assumption of our capitalist culture has almost always been the reverse—that labor is for the sake of capital, i.e. that it is profits that count, whatever may happen to the workers. But the religious bodies are now in increasing agreement that the most important thing in the whole tangle of economic life is *what happens to people.* If a splendid product is being produced, but people are being destroyed by the working conditions under which it is produced, or are paid such exploitively low wages that they cannot support themselves and their families, the situation must be condemned and then corrected.

It was to redress such injustices, of course, that working people first began to organize, and it is gratifying to discover that contemporary religious bodies see this as an authentic moral struggle and not (as it is often perceived by the rest of society) as the selfish attempt of one "special interest group" to take advantage of the others.

The situation, of course, is always volatile. There is continual need for fresh appraisal, for responses to new forms of exploitation, and for creating structures that embody more and more justice rather than less and less. If theory and practice were in true harmony, the religious organizations, which in their pronouncements uphold labor's right to organize, would place their substantial moral and legislative influence behind labor law reform. For example, repeal of the Taft-Hartley "right to work" laws has been on the legislative agenda of labor for many years, but unions need allies in this legislative fight and would welcome the tangible assistance of the churches. More immediately, reform of the National Labor Relations Act (NLRA) to provide for more rapid elections, reduce delays, and provide for mandatory recognition and bargaining based upon showing a majority interest in a union is urgently needed. There is significant data in the work of Medoff and Freeman, cited above, that the decline of unionization is directly related to an increase of employers' unfair labor practices. And there are numerous instances in which corporations retain law firms whose objectives are to decertify unions where they exist, and prevent unions from organizing where workers are seeking representation. (This is true even within some large religious bodies, as we shall presently see.) Another "new" area in which alliances are needed is in the attempt to pass legislation that mandates corporations to give advance notice of plant closings, both for the sake of the workers to be laid off, and for the ongoing economic stability of the areas in which the closings occur. As of this writing modest proposals for such notice are in various federal and state legislative processes, and the needs are such that one should be able to look for significant joint lobbying by labor and religious groups.

Some Further Coalitions

The issue of plant closings is only the most recent reminder that there are other areas cited in the political and economic justice statements in which religious bodies and working people could be cooperating. Let us note a few of them.

Unemployment, for example, rather than inflation, needs to be recognized as the primary problem—an emphasis that the Canadian Roman Catholic bishops develop explicitly. Full employment at adequate pay with satisfactory working conditions is a *basic right for all* (not just a privilege for a few), and it must be worked for by both unions and churches. Failure to forge a common alliance and lobbying effort on this matter leads to injustice for all.

Most of the documents under consideration speak specifically of the need to strengthen the family. This is not being proposed from the perspective of such groups as Moral Majority, who want to reaffirm "traditional values" in such a way as to get women out of the work force, but from a perspective that affirms that such things as education, housing, health care and a decent income for all are, once again, *basic rights for all* (not just privileges for a few). Churches need to help clarify the fact that when unions lobby for such goals as these they are not simply acting out of selfish concern for a "special interest group," but expressing a concern for the basic human rights of everyone within the society. The same dynamic is at work when unions are lobbying for a higher minimum wage, a national health service, better schools, and child care at the workplace. Religious bodies who agree that these must be human possibilities available for everyone should not only issue statements, but lend their institutional support (and clout) to all sectors of society who share such a vision. A number of the documents deal with health care for the elderly and policies that will provide for retirement with dignity. These are perceived by many church groups as rights that follow from their recognition that all people, without exception, are created in God's image. Whether that vocabulary is used or not, it is true that unions also work for these ends, and they often already have retirement plans and health care benefits that are providing such services for their members. They would agree that such services appropriately belong to all persons and would welcome an opportunity to be allies with religious bodies in lobbying for their extension. Since many union pensioners are already active in religious organizations, the necessary connections would not be hard to establish.

On many other areas of broad social concern, unions and religious bodies are already in substantial agreement. Most of them agree about the necessity of cuts in defense spending and diversion of some of the funds saved into programs for economic conversion. The same is true on many environmental issues, and on food and agriculture policy, concerning which a number of religious statements speak in detail. And from whatever perspective, there is agreement that significant tax reform is needed. Working people are particularly aware of the ways in which they have been forced to carry an unfairly large portion of the tax burden. And even though there has recently been "tax reform" legislation, it is already clear that while this alters the appearance of the tax structure, the biases still favor wealthy individuals and large corporations. Here is where pushing the presumed "self-interest" of workers would actually promote a tax structure more closely approximating "justice for all."

A Challenge to the Churches

Thus we see that there are many points in these documents with which labor can agree and even express gratitude for the ways in which various religious bodies, in words at least, support the rights and needs of working people. That there are major disparities between these visions and the actualities of the American scene can be taken for granted, and, as has been suggested, churches and unions could make common cause in supporting many specific programs that would bring the dream and the reality closer together.

But there is a further matter on which unions, while concerned about setting their own houses in order in response to criticism, must issue a similar challenge to the churches. Those of us who work for labor unions frequently discover that our attempts to organize workers and set up systems of collective bargaining within the churches themselves are met by strenuous opposition from within those very church structures. Not only is union-busting a major growth industry in the country at large (with resources estimated at over $250,000,000 a year along with several thousand management consultants and lawyers), but it has invaded the churches as well. Monsignor George Higgins recently described a major Catholic hospital in which a union organizing drive was underway among the staff. The hospital president sent a memo to all employees urging them to vote non-union. That may have been his individual right, but the memo appeared to have been drafted by a union-busting management consultant, since it used language characteristic of all such attempts, describing union representatives indiscriminately as "shoddy third-party . . . outsiders," and charging the union with "coercion, corruption and violence" as well as "hypocrisy." It contrasted the blessings of the workers' "individual independence" to the grim specter of union "collectivism," and concluded that the hospital intended "to do everything legally possible to oppose any union getting in here." (See Higgins, "Union Busting Counters Church Stand," in *Conference Report,* p. 8.)

In another major archdiocese, the church retains a law firm for counsel that has used every stalling tactic known to prevent elections, prolong non-recognition of the union before and after election victories, and maintain a disruptive influence in labor relations. It has also, over a period of many years, supported such unacceptable bargaining positions as to force a number of strikes by members of my own local. (For a fully documented account of these and other tactics, see the report "Littler, Mendelson, Fastiff and Tichy: A Law Firm Operating in 'Labor Relations'," by Ellen Teninty, available from the Center for Ethics and Social Policy, 2400 Ridge Road, Berkeley, CA 94709.)

In the Protestant world there have been similar disparities between the theoretical right of workers to organize, and massive institutional opposition, when actual workers began to try to organize within the church structures themselves. A number of years ago the leadership of the National Council of Churches (the largest interdenominational Protestant body and one which has had a good track record, on paper, of supporting the right of workers to organize) successfully brought strong enough pressures to bear on its own employees so that a drive to unionize the Council offices was defeated.

Fortunately there is increasing recognition within such religious bodies that internal gaps between utterance and performance must be overcome if their message is to be taken seriously by others. Only as they put their own houses in order can churches expect their exhortations to others to be taken seriously. A significant acknowledgement of this fact is contained in the concluding chapter of the Roman Catholic bishops' letter on the economy, especially in the section on "The Church as Economic Actor." The bishops recognize that *"All the moral principles that govern the just operation of any economic endeavor apply to the Church and its agencies and institutions; indeed the Church should be exemplary"* (p. 174; italics in original).

Labor will wait with hope to see these words transformed into deeds.

Looking to the Future

As we look to the political future of our country and ask which way organized labor is going, it should not be hard to see why labor unions gave such strong support to Jesse Jackson in the Democratic primaries of 1988, and why support for him can be expected to build in the future. The question of true participatory democracy was addressed by Jackson through the massive voter registration campaigns that he conducted in both the 1984 and 1988 primaries, and their recognition that all citizens should have access to decision-making power. It was Jackson who consistently spoke about empowering people, minorities, women, the young, old and disabled. He was campaigning against drug dealers and drug users long before other major candidates saw this as an election year issue. Similarly he has fought for equal education and equal access to education, universal health care, affordable housing, and help for the family farmer. He is the only candidate who has walked union picket lines and recognized that multinational corporations and corporate capital have devastated our industries and our ability to compete. On the international level he has consistently worked toward peace and disavowed our enormous appetite for defense spending and the granting of foreign aid based upon weapons rather than capital investment and food. In the light of such a track record, then, it is not surprising that Jackson has had, and will continue to have, strong union support in the years ahead.

In addition to such specific advocacy, there are two broader political issues with which labor will be concerned in the future. What labor really requires for its own voice to be heard—given that it claims to speak for a majority of American working people —is a political party of its own. Such a party would have candidates who come from the broad diversity of organized workplaces, who recognize the needs of working people, who will remain constant on issues of social and economic justice, and who will not incur political debts to "special interest" groups.

All that may be a long way off in the future, and until that time workers must forge coalitions with all sectors of society in order to bring about the kinds of changes with which this book is concerned. At that time our coalitions will have become organic parts of our society and give direction to a different form of political party. When that happens, a truly democratic majority will formulate and conduct domestic and foreign policy in line with the interests of the majority rather than the minority, and working people everywhere will be the beneficiaries.

8. Third World Perspectives: A View from Below

Julia Estrella and Walden Bello

Racial/ethnic communities in the United States and people in the third world would undoubtedly view the appearance of the denominational statements under discussion in this book as a positive development. The documents are particularly useful in describing certain dimensions of the current economic crisis— the spreading poverty and increasing inequality in the United States, the escalating third world debt crisis, and the growing, devastating misery of the third world.

Our role, however, is not simply to celebrate, but, more importantly, to provide a constructive critique that will help clarify the tasks at hand. The documents do indeed sound the alarm, but their collective shortcoming is that they do not follow this up with a clear analysis of the *causes* of the problem, perhaps out of apprehension about the course of action that might be prescribed by such an analysis.

Tiptoeing Around the Core Issues: Exploitation and Underdevelopment

Consider, for instance, the statement of the United Church of Christ. After offering a sweeping view of poverty and underdevelopment in the third world, the writers ask:

> Are people in less developed countries poor because they are exploited by United States-owned multinational corporations? Multinational corporations pay significantly lower wages and provide fewer, if any, benefits in these countries than in similar facilities in the industrial-

105

ized countries. Their levels of remuneration, however, usually compare quite favorably with indigenous wages and working conditions. Therefore, millions of unemployed and underemployed people in the Third World are seeking jobs in a multinational corporation. As Joan Robinson, a British economist, once remarked, the only thing worse than being exploited is not to be exploited at all and to be unemployed.[1]

Admittedly, underdevelopment is not a simple phenomenon to understand or explain, and there are many contributing factors. But what we seek in a document on economic justice is a clear stand on the main causes of underdevelopment, not an analysis that disperses responsibility for a tragedy, and ultimately attributes it to the impersonal world-historic process of the "emergence of a global economy."

The realization, so clear to those taking "a view from below," that the transnational corporations are, for the most part, engines of exploitation and underdevelopment is not a realization that will come from reading the UCC document. But the UCC document is not alone. Consider the statement of the U.S. Catholic bishops. After providing a panoramic view of the devastating consequences of transnational capital's search for cheap labor, the bishops shrink back from the analytical and ethical implications of the picture they have drawn:

> Such inequitable consequences, however, are not necessary consequences of transnational corporate activity. Corporations can contribute to development by attracting and training high-caliber managers and other personnel, by helping organize effective marketing systems, by generating additional capital, by introducing or reinforcing financial accountability and by sharing the knowledge gained from their own research and development activities.[2]

In a position paper on economic justice, the point is not to produce a neutral, "even-handed" statement, but to assume a clear partisan stance that uncompromisingly lays out the prime causes of poverty and inequality.

One document does make the analytic breakthrough, but it does not come from a United States denomination. Perhaps it is because the Canadian Catholic bishops come from a country dominated by the United States that they were able to articulate so clearly the core problem in both the developed and the underdeveloped world:

> The basic social contradiction of our times is the structural domination of capital and technology over people, over labor, over communities. What is required is a radical inversion of these relationships. In other words, ways must be found for people to exercise more effective control over both capital and technology so they become constructive instruments of creation by serving the basic needs of people and communities.[3]

Capitalism is the problem, the bishops tell us, and as they consider the possibility of an alternative, they are also much more forthright than the Americans (even though their stand has drawn accusations of being "pro-socialist"):

> If communities are going to develop their resources to serve basic human and social needs, it is essential that they have effective control over the kinds of capital and technology required to achieve these objectives. If working people are going to exercise their right to become subjects of production, then new forms of worker-controlled industries need to be developed.[4]

The Debt Crisis: Obscuring Responsibility

The analytical ambivalence that envelops the American denominations' discussion of the core problems is extended to two stress points in the relationship between the north and the south: the debt crisis and the aid relationship. Let us examine them in turn.

The documents deal in a confused fashion with the origins of the massive trillion dollar debt that the third world owes western and Japanese financial institutions. Statements by the Catholic bishops and the Disciples of Christ, for example, list the Soviet Union's buying of U.S. grain, and OPEC's oil pricing policies, as causes of the present debt crisis, in addition to the profit-seeking of the big banks. The UCC statement faults the deterioration of the prices of third world exports relative to their imports, and the third world countries themselves for borrowing large sums from western banks.

We do not deny that such factors have contributed to the development of the crisis, but when they are presented as part of a grocer's list of causes of the crisis, the result is confusion and dispersal of responsibility. Because their massive purchases inadvertently raised grain prices, the Soviets are made out to be just as responsible for the crisis as the New York banks!

The debt crisis was *not* produced by a chance concatenation of events, as the documents under consideration imply. As one top Bank of America executive admitted, "the greed of bankers" was central to the process.[5]

Even before the OPEC price rise of 1973, the big New York banks were lending to third world countries, owing to the declining profitability of their operations in the metropolitan countries. By 1973, for instance, bank lending to third world countries had already reached $22.7 billion.[6] In other words, the OPEC money of $155 billion deposited in western banks between 1974 and 1980 was channeled by the banks to an *already existing,* and profitable, pattern of lending. The banks talked about "responsibly recycling" OPEC cash, a statement that smacks more of ideology than of altruism. The prospect of massive profits was the driving force, and Citibank's Walter Wriston led the way with his theory about how countries were better credit risks than companies because, unlike the latter, countries never go bankrupt.[7]

Implying that banks loaned to the third world at large is not really accurate, for lending was concentrated in a few countries. In addition to Mexico, the preferred customers were Brazil, Argentina, Chile, South Korea, and the Philippines. A common characteristic of the latter countries throughout the 1970s and early 1980s was that they were ruled by military-technocratic elites. The surface "stability" of an authoritarian order, in other words, provided the bankers with the reassurance that their loans would be repaid. This bias toward dictatorships was further strengthened by institutional similarities between banks and dictatorships. As one high level Bank of America official said:

> Authoritarian governments appealed to the bank manager who, after all, came from an institution with basically authoritarian structures. It was like dealing with somebody like a CEO [chief executive officer] at the other end of the table. It was so attractive—people like Delfim Netto [of Brazil] came across as standing for unifying the country, no politics, and stability. They were good CEOs.[8]

The debt crisis did not stem from third world countries living beyond their means, as conventional wisdom would have it. It was the product of a peculiar alliance of international bankers, military elites, technocrats, and local financial operators. Massive lending by the big banks sparked a peculiar kind of hothouse speculative capitalism, with its own division of labor: the *technocrats* would conjure up grandiose development projects to justify massive financing, the *generals* would divert part of the cash to Mirage jets and Exocet missiles, and the *finance* men would immediately transmit much of the capital back to New York and Geneva, not as repayments but as deposits in personal accounts—often in the same money-center banks that had made the loans. Massive lending and capital flight went hand in hand, and for a time the New York banks were profiting handsomely from both operations.

The International Monetary Fund (IMF) and the World Bank, the two western-controlled agencies that monitor international capital flow, had a role in creating this crisis. In their third world lending, the private banks depended a lot on the IMF's and World Bank's estimates of a country's credit-worthiness. Contrary to its image of being an impartial watchdog over third world finances, the IMF made exceptions based on ideological considerations.

Invariably, the favored governments were strongly pro-western, anti-communist authoritarian regimes that were considered strategic allies by Washington. Invariably, too, evidence of massive capital flight, waste, and mismanagement was systematically overlooked by the Fund and the Bank.

For instance, until the assassination of Marcos' rival, Benigno Aquino, in 1983, the IMF consistently gave the Marcos regime an A-1 credit rating, while the World Bank lobbied for foreign investment to locate there because, as Bank internal papers put it, the Philippines had "a strong absorptive capacity for foreign capital."

We have devoted considerable space to elucidating the prime cause of the debt crisis in order to build a case for the position that repudiation of the debt is a just course of action. In most of the denominational statements, debt relief is proposed as an act of Christian charity, i.e. "debt forgiveness," whereas it would actually be a blow for *justice* on behalf of the vast majority of the people of indebted countries, who not only had no part in the decisions of bankers and dictators that led to the massive indebtedness in the first place, but also derived no benefits from them.

With debt repudiation being ethically justified, the vital questions become practical ones: Is unilateral debt repudiation a tactically feasible course of action for a third world country? Can it make such a policy stick without drawing such massive retaliation from the banks and the United States that the result would be even more economic chaos? What are the possibilities for coordinated action among debtor countries to tip the balance of power against the creditors?

The point is that the church documents are not comfortable with such scenarios of appropriate confrontation and conflict initiated by the oppressed. In the debt issue as elsewhere, the appeal continues to be to the charity and reasonableness of the banks and the rich. It soon becomes apparent that the documents are written primarily for the elites and the middle class, not the poor, the oppressed and the minorities.

Aid as Obstacle

In addition to the debt crisis, the issue of aid is a second area shrouded in analytical obscurity. Nearly all the documents adopt the "liberal" line of urging the United States to increase its development aid. The Catholic bishops' statement is representative:

> We are dismayed that the U.S., once a pioneer in foreign aid, is almost last among the 17 industrialized nations in the Organization for Economic Cooperation and Development in percentage of gross national product devoted to aid. Reduction of the U.S. contribution to multilateral development institutions is particularly regrettable, because these institutions are often better able than the bilateral agencies to focus on the poor and reduce dependency in developing countries.[9]

From the point of view of developing countries, however, the issue is not really the amount of aid given but the *conditions and objectives* of foreign aid. Western aid is often tied to purchases of goods from the donor country. It is usually aimed at promoting private enterprises that will exhibit a high rate of return to investment. Most of the time, the aid is funneled through and coordinated by governments; this not only strengthens and legitimizes authoritarian and oligarchical regimes, but also provides innumerable opportunities for corruption. Also, western aid is often aimed at increasing productivity through technological advance without altering existing inequalities in political and economic power. Finally, aid often serves as the forerunner of foreign investment, laying down the physical and social infrastructure to facilitate the effective penetration of a country by transnational capital.[10]

The relationship between the Philippines and the World Bank is a classical illustration of aid policies that aggravate rather than alleviate underdevelopment—contrary to the Catholic bishops' unfounded belief in the superiority of multilateral aid.[11]

During the fourteen years of the Marcos dictatorship, the Philippines received about $4 billion in aid from the World Bank. This aid, however, was accompanied by policy prescriptions and biases that inflicted penalties on the recipient country. For instance, the Bank management's preference for a centralized, technocratic management of the development process helped consolidate the Marcos dictatorship. The Bank's advice to Marcos to attract foreign investors by offering the bait of cheap labor clearly contributed to the depression in the living standards of Filipino workers throughout the Marcos period. By focusing its projects on raising productivity without altering unequal patterns of land ownership, the Bank helped to widen and entrench economic inequality. As the Bank acknowledged in an internal memo:

> A substantial portion of agricultural growth . . . was concentrated in activities known to have substantial commercial content, and one could therefore argue that the benefits from the high level of agricultural growth may not have reached substantial numbers of the poor.[12]

Indeed, the percentage of Filipino families living below the government-defined poverty line *increased* between the beginning of the dictatorship and the end of the Marcos regime from forty-eight to sixty-three percent.

The argument should not be misinterpreted: aid for emergency relief during periods of natural calamity is crucially important. But development aid should only be given if it can clearly be proven to empower people at the grassroots. Otherwise, no aid is better than some aid.

At this point, our two areas of investigation are seen to overlap. *Aid* is often used to obscure the need of the indebted countries for *debt repudiation*. The Philippines, for instance, received $1 billion in aid in 1987, yet it paid out $2 billion in interest payments—making it a net capital exporter to the tune of $1 billion. In the last five years, the difference between the outflow of debt service payments from, and fresh foreign capital inflows into, all indebted third world countries was negative and massive—over $140 billion!

A hemorrhage of third world resources is taking place before our eyes, and the churches have not acknowledged it. Our conclusion: debt repudiation, not aid, is today the *conditio sine qua non* of genuine development in the third world.

Supporting Confrontation and Involving the Poor

A key element of the churches' economic policy toward the third world must be to support unilateral or coordinated actions of debt repudiation by indebted countries. Other parts of such a program might include (a) backing moves to alter radically the character and agenda of foreign aid, and (b) participating in international efforts to restrict the mobility and power of transnational capital, especially U.S. capital. These efforts must be part of a larger global agenda, the centerpiece of which would be coordinated solidarity actions between workers and minorities in the north and the nations of the south.

The North American churches cannot be expected to assume leadership in this process. But they can be asked to support confrontational actions by the oppressed, since the hour for polite negotiated solutions with the rich is long past.

If economic justice statements are really to serve as agenda for action by the churches, they must avoid the obfuscation of established abstract economic theory, and acknowledge forthrightly the systematic impoverishment, exploitation, and alienation created on a world scale by capitalism and imperialism. (Contemporary socialist governments have their own analogous shortcomings, but they must not become an excuse for ignoring the massive tragedies spawned by western capitalism and U.S. imperialism.) For poor people, both here and in the third world, oppression and exploitation are realities, not just theoretical constructs.

This means that it is imperative that in the future the poor and the oppressed be actively integrated into the creation of policy statements by religious bodies. It will no longer be enough for the rich to speak "on behalf of the poor." The voice of the poor must be heard directly. This will ensure that middle and upper-middle income church people who read the statements are exposed to the real world as experienced by the poor and oppressed. Many will choose not to "hear," but there will be some who will experience confession and conversion and be moved to action.

Bringing the poor into the drafting process would also guarantee that the statements truly become springboards for relevant action. For as economic justice papers become increasingly popular, there is a tendency for words to become a substitute for action, and we are in danger of being swamped by a flood of "moral visions." We need to recall that in the brief time of Jesus' ministry, he spent no time writing. Instead, he went around the countryside preaching, teaching, healing and casting out demons. He demanded resolute action from his followers, free of intellectual vacillation or ethical qualifications. Confronted by him today, our churches are asked to respond decisively like Zacchaeus, who, when similarly confronted by Jesus, did not say, "I will chair a committee to examine the tax structure of Galilee," but rather said, "I give half of my wealth to the poor; and if I have taken anything from any man falsely, I will restore him fourfold." And Jesus responded, "Today salvation has come to this house" (cf. Lk 19:1–10).

Notes

1. *Christian Faith and Economic Life: A Study Paper Contributing to a Pronouncement for the Seventeenth General Synod of the United Church of Christ* (New York: United Church Board for World Ministries, 1987), p. 20. Hereafter to be referred to as UCC Statement.

2. U.S. Catholic Bishops, *Economic Justice for All: Catholic Social Teaching and the U.S. Economy* (Washington, D.C.: NC Documentary Service, 1986), p. 439.

3. Canada Conference of Catholic Bishops, *Ethical and Political Challenges* (Ottawa: Canada Conference of Catholic Bishops, 1983), p. 14.

4. *Ibid.,* p. 17.

5. Lewis Coleman, Bank of America vice president for international lending, Statement at forum on "International Debt and Economic Justice for All." Santa Clara University, Santa Clara, California, May 6, 1987.

6. For a fuller discussion of this interpretation of events, see Walden Bello and Claudio Saunt, "International Debt Crisis, Year Five," *Christianity and Crisis,* November 23, 1987, pp. 403–413.

7. Walter Wriston, cited in Bernard Nossiter, *The Global Struggle for More* (New York: Harper and Row, 1987), p. 6.

8. Interview with high Bank of America executive who wishes to remain anonymous, conducted by Walden Bello and Claudio Saunt, San Francisco, June 26, 1987.

9. U.S. Catholic bishops, p. 437.

10. For a fuller discussion, see Frances Moore Lappe, Joseph Collins, and David Kinley, *Aid as Obstacle* (San Francisco: Food First, 1981).

11. The following discussion is drawn from Walden Bello, Elaine Elinson, and David Kinley, *Development Debacle: The World Bank in the Philippines* (San Francisco: Food First, 1982).

12. World Bank, "Poverty, Basic Needs, and Employment," Confidential draft, Washington, D.C., January 1980, p. 158.

PART IV

MOVING FROM STATEMENTS TO ACTION: A VARIETY OF PROPOSALS

9. A Vision
Requires a Strategy

Loni Hancock

About ten years ago I began to believe that until a profound shift occurred in the values by which we evaluate economic choices, few hopeful or interesting changes would be possible in politics. Such issues as how long people work, for what wages, at what kinds of production, and under what physical and psychological conditions determine most of what else is possible in their lives. Therefore, if we care about the quality of human life, we must become involved with economic policy.

The statements on the economy by religious groups that we are considering in this book have the potential to bring about that shift in evaluating economic alternatives. In a situation in which economic debate has for many years been narrowly confined to the "market-oriented" portion of the spectrum of options, they can restore a desperately needed balance. They come at an opportune moment in history, because in the next decade we will have to restructure our national economy, in the context of the realities of an emerging global economy in which we will play the unenviable role of largest debtor nation.

As the mayor of a middle-sized American city, facing all the problems of American cities everywhere—from potholes to unemployment and child care to drug abuse—I find the ideas in these documents a breath of fresh air and hope in a musty closet. The question is whether they will come out of the closet and onto the street and into the rough and tumble of the struggle for the hearts and minds of the American people. This is the major challenge of the documents.

The business of turning ideas into policy and policy into reality is what I have spent most of my adult life thinking about and doing. In this chapter, therefore, rather than refer in detail to the content of the documents I will share some reflections and experiences that may be useful to members of the religious community as they take the ideas set out in the documents and seek to move them into the mainstream of public debate.

The documents demand that we rethink our definitions of a "successful economy." In the prevailing paradigm, the opportunity for individual wealth is the factor of over-riding importance in making individual and social economic choices. By contrast, the religious statements suggest other factors of importance that fit into a longer-term concept of self-interest: a planet with undepleted resources to leave our children; a country with education and health care for all; a world without extremes of wealth, so that no one is so poor or so envious as to feel compelled to steal; a society that encourages human dignity by providing opportunities to make a social contribution and still have adequate income and enough time for leisure and intimacy.

To take on the task of economic rebuilding successfully, we can be helped by applying the insights of the great psychologists who were deeply concerned with the human spirit: Jung, with his insistence of the need for balance in human life; Erikson, with his assessment of the opportunities for growth; Maslow, with his hierarchy of needs beginning with physical security and culminating in what he called "self-actualization," the search for ways to use all our capacities fully.

In watching the life of my own community, I have come to believe that after an adequate level of food and shelter is secured, life may be better enhanced by increasing opportunities for experience, rather than for the making of more money.

"Experience" can take many forms, ranging from adventure and artistic expression to intimacy and play. The current emphasis on money as the only important economic good has had frightening social consequences. Last year's headlines about stockbrokers making millions selling junk bonds, and promoting non-productive mergers of companies, indicate to our children that what is done is not as important as what makes money. I have had youngsters look me in the eye and say: "But why should I work for $3.50 an hour at McDonalds, when I can make $50 an hour as a lookout for drug pushers?" How can we be surprised and horrified when less advantaged Americans see selling drugs as their way to get rich quick, if "getting rich quick" is promoted by the establishment as all that matters?

It is ironic that for most of the world the first step in the Maslow hierarchy of needs—security, food and shelter—is still the major challenge. It is a global task, and we in this country could help tremendously by living simply, so that others may simply live. The prevailing paradigm with its emphasis on money—but only for some—offers little in the way of hope and certainly does not challenge the best and most idealistic energies in any of us.

Even for the privileged, the prevailing paradigm appears to be a frantic struggle for personal financial success with little time for the non-material self and little support from the impoverished public sector. It is a struggle in which greed and envy are encouraged by pervasive advertising that plays to the most petty aspects of human nature. It is a race in which there is no such thing as "enough." It has led to a national economy that increasingly resembles an hour-glass—with many wealthy beyond the wildest imaginings of people in other nations and other historical periods, many more who are barely hanging on at the edges of poverty, and a small and squeezed middle class.

As a person who works in the secular political world, I am struck by how profoundly this two-tier economy undermines not only religious values but democratic ones as well. Democracy is a system that seems to thrive in societies where a strong middle class makes up the majority of people. This demands a system of economic arrangements that can provide jobs and income for most people at a level that leads to security, self-reliance and the ability to become partners in working toward the common good of the community.

Democracy has not fared well in nations, such as many in Latin America, where there is still great division between rich and poor. This is troubling because economists tell us that our economy is beginning to look like that which we associate with underdeveloped nations—absentee-owned plantation/corporate agriculture replacing the family farmer, multinationally-owned corporations (with allegiance to no particular spot on earth or its people) replacing the Jeffersonian vision of the independent economic factor, farmer or merchant, rooted in a sense of place, and, at every point, great extremes of wealth. It is unclear whether democracy can thrive in the long term under these conditions.

Given the immense costs of modern political campaigns, and the fact that most campaign contributions come from businesses and corporations with immediate legislative self-interests, it may also be naive to think that if a few control the economic system everyone will control the political system. In spite of the increasing use of the most seductive technologies of modern advertising, the United States has the lowest voting rate of any democracy in the world. This should lead us to question whether our social contract, our sense of connectedness to each other and society, does not need renewing and revitalizing, and whether political democracy in the long term may not depend on achieving an economic democracy in the next decade.

Into this situation and set of dilemmas the documents under consideration assert the need and appropriateness of moral vision and the existence of legitimate motivations beyond the purely financial. They open the possibility of what E. M. Schumacher has called "economics as if people mattered." They take the notion of the sacredness of human life out of the church and into the marketplace—a giant and daring step!

Although the documents differ in style and degree of specificity, their outlines of a new way of looking at the economy are strikingly clear. Rather than individual competition and individual gain, their new paradigm is based on notions of equity and community. They reaffirm that we are all fundamentally in each other's care, and that there is a sacred, non-quantifiable dimension to human life which must be acknowledged and accommodated in any set of economic arrangements.

Are the Documents Realistic?

If there is anything I have learned after many years of political work at many levels of government, it is that "realism" is in the eye of the beholder. Ideas that are quite sensible and correct are often dismissed as "unrealistic" when what is meant is that in the opinion of the listener, they do not have a constituency and therefore cannot be implemented.

We must never confuse "unrealistic-because-no-one-wants-it" with "unrealistic" as "inherently unworkable." C. Wright Mills, the famous sociologist, coined the term "crackpot realism" to describe the very human tendency to cling to courses of action that are clearly disastrous on the grounds that they are in keeping with the prevailing wisdom and therefore "realistic."

The documents under consideration, and particularly the statement by the Roman Catholic bishops, say what honest economists have known for years—that economics is not a cosmic force with natural laws that must be discovered and obeyed, but a set of tools that can be used to fashion any set of social arrangements human beings find compelling. If individual wealth is the goal, a set of arrangements can be fashioned to assure wealth for a few. If the opportunity for a fully realized life for all people regardless of economic circumstances is the goal, that goal too is achievable, but will require a different set of economic techniques. In the end, "we the people" decide what we want—or how much of what we don't want we will put up with.

How can we tell a successful economy from a failed economy? That depends on our goals. It is important for all readers of this book to define for themselves what they believe a successful economy would look like. Only then can it be decided whether present policies are realistic and adequate, or whether they need to be changed.

In *Alice in Wonderland,* the Cheshire Cat tells Alice, "If you don't know where you're going, any road will take you there." The value of the religious documents on the economy is that they propose human-centered criteria for evaluating the economy, allow us to contrast them with prevailing paradigms, and encourage us to define signposts and destinations that will put us on the road to where we really want to go.

How Do We Get There?

The documents we are examining are eloquent and certainly helpful. The big question, of course, is: *How* helpful? It is still unclear whether they will be able to galvanize enough social and political energy to make implementation possible. In politics, and in the churches, it's what gets done after the eloquent statement is written that makes the difference. A vision without a strategy is merely a pipedream.

My experience in political life has persuaded me that there are two factors that define the degree of seriousness with which elected people approach ideas and programs. They are *constituency* and *money*. Both are essential to get elected and re-elected in a democratic system.

Because of the need to be closely in touch with the electorate, elected officials rarely move ideas from the fringes of public debate to center stage as "ideas-in-good-currency." Elected people are more likely to propose legislation that will institutionalize ideas for which there is already significant public demand.

Only when the crisis is of such overwhelming proportions that the outcry for almost *any* solution becomes overwhelming can elected people risk getting out in front with specific solutions that are unfamiliar. For example, limited equity cooperative housing is a unique way to build moderate income housing; individuals have the tax and tenure advantages of home ownership, and although they do not build equity, costs can be kept low for succeeding tenants. Berkeley pioneered the first limited-equity coops in this country in the 1970s, when I was a council member. It was a new idea, and there was a fight for every dollar of seed money the city provided. Only the community demand for affordable housing made this idea one whose time had finally come.

On such issues, constituency can be measured in numbers and in passion. A small group of people totally committed to achieving a goal can have an enormous impact in a democratic system. Usually, in fact, it is the work of a passionate and dedicated minority that finally leads to massive shifts in public opinion. When there is such a sea-change in a community's sense of what is possible and appropriate, it invariably and inexorably will lead to implementing legislation.

An environmentalist friend remarked that "the day may come when we will look at the private ownership of irreplaceable natural resources the way we now look with horror at the idea of one human being owning another." The environmental movement in America is a prime example of how the community sense of what should be constantly changes, as ideas move "into-good-currency" and finally into application. Polls by Mervyn Field indicate that after twenty years of education and organizing, over eighty percent of the people in the state of California now identify themselves as environmentalists. That's a long way from the first "Earth Days" of the late 1960s.

In the light of all this, as we consider the potential impact of the church documents on the economy, we must ask if there is the passion and the will to connect these inspiring values and inherently realistic public policy goals with the world of implementation—that is, with education, advocacy and politics. If not, they will remain beautiful statements of inspiration to occasional readers, but become little else. However, if implementation is the goal, it is important to plan a strategy for getting the ideas and programs in the statements before the public, and ultimately before the legislative bodies that can institutionalize them.

Learning from the Political World:
A Five Step Program

Just as the documents represent a marked departure from traditional ways of thinking about the economy, so active economic advocacy would be a marked departure from traditional church-state relationships. Religious organizations have usually refrained from direct advocacy of economic and political programs. A notable and successful exception has been the civil rights movement, which combined spiritual vision and political action, until the collective sense of the possible did indeed enlarge, change and get codified into law.

In economics, as in civil rights, we need leaders and passionate educators who share a dream, can talk inspiringly about the dream and are willing to devote their lives to the achievement of that dream. If the churches and synagogues are willing to take on the challenge of restoring an ethical dimension to economics, there are a series of steps they must take if they wish to achieve significant policy change in any arena.

1. Public Recognition of the Problem

This initial point sounds obvious but it is crucial and often not done well. For perfectly understandable reasons, human beings generally prefer the stable and the familiar. "Problems" must be given names, recognized, and deplored, so that human energy and adrenalin can be mustered to overcome the inevitable bias toward the status quo.

In the 1960s we had a tremendous problem in Berkeley with police brutality, directed toward young people and people of color. The greatest obstacle to confronting and dealing with it was the refusal of the city council to acknowledge that anything more was wrong than "one or two bad apples" on the police force. It was not until a local Baptist minister was beaten that a *systemic* problem was recognized and a policy adopted to correct it. Today our police force is quite different. It is integrated racially and sexually and has an increasing emphasis on community policing. We can hardly remember the problem that once absorbed so much of our energy.

In the economic arena, analogously, if people do not understand such problems as (a) the dangers of the national deficit and the international debt, (b) the widening income gap between rich and poor, or (c) the destruction of natural resources for the short-term financial gain of a few individuals, we will never develop an energized and searching public ready to look at old situations in new ways.

2. Defining Alternatives

Once there is recognition that the system is, in fact, broken, we can begin asking how it can be fixed. What we need at this stage are strong positive models of successful economic arrangements. These can take the form of theoretical or fictional writings, or real-life comparisons of how economies work in other areas of this country or the globe.

Much of our present confusion stems from cumulative folk wisdom that says that only "the market" can generate the incredible wealth of industrialized nations today, that all can attain it if they are smart and work hard, and that nations with an active public sector are invariably uncreative and impoverished.

A real comparison of the economy of the United States with that of other developed nations leads to the opposite conclusion. Most industrialized nations have a strong public sector including active government partnerships with major industries and labor. Extensive and excellent state systems ensure education and health care for all. Japan and western Europe have lower infant mortality rates and crime rates and higher standards of living than we do. Our citizens should ask whether they do not have a right to as high a standard of living, and as much security and opportunity, as citizens in countries whose military budgets are being subsidized by our country.

3. Developing Programs

Here is the part of the process that economists enjoy—figuring out exactly how to arrange the health care system, or the tax system, or the ways of building and allocating housing. If economics is seen as a tool rather than as a set of immutable laws, the human genius that has taken us into space can be counted on to maintain us on the earth with an ample supply of both bread and roses.

4. Building a Constituency

This step requires a combination of broad-based education and inspiration. Constituency-building allows leaders with an analysis and program to say to their fellow citizens, "Can you see what I see?" The ability to enlist support for a shared vision is the key to successful social change.

There are several audiences that must be reached by the leaders of any emerging movement. One audience is *opinionmakers,* those who can reach others and certify that an idea is "thinkable." Another audience is the *grassroots,* the not-so-ordinary people whose support is essential if the idea is to be successfully implemented.

Often it is the opinion-makers for whom the system presently works fairly well. It is no accident that power-brokers and many elected officials oppose public financing of elections, since that would open up to others the system that put them in office. It is no accident that the most profound social movements have been those in which the committed early leadership has gone directly to the people feeling the problem and inspired them with hope and resolve.

In the 1960s, my next door neighbor, Ed Roberts, a quadriplegic since a bout with polio in his early teens, insisted on being admitted to the University of California in spite of well-meaning doctors explaining that as a "hopeless cripple" he couldn't possibly succeed. Ed started the international movement for, and by, the physically disabled, from his iron lung and motorized wheelchair. Today, thanks to Ed and the thousands that came to share his vision, our attitudes toward physical disability have completely turned around, and we have found that the "unrealistic" is indeed perfectly possible.

Any new movement produces its own leaders. The role of elected officials is to encourage them and work with them to get the message out, while translating the vision into programs and ultimately into legislation.

5. Implementation

This is generally done through legislation and public policy change. However, we should note that many profound social changes have been institutionalized simply through the multiplication of individual decisions to change personal behavior.

Changes in the status of women, for example, are largely the result of a series of private decisions that have resulted in a completely reshaped family and work life. In the civil rights and peace movements, on the other hand, people confronted and frequently disobeyed policies they considered profoundly wrong, as a last resort, when people's sense of themselves and their securities are deeply threatened. Both kinds of implementation, however, depend in the end on public policy catching up through legislation.

Most *economic policy* changes depend solely on legislation since they tend to involve organizational rather than individual decisions. When our tax policies or health care policies no longer work we seek new forms of organization and regulation that require formal policy decisions.

The economic debate seldom seems to touch people's lives in the immediate and emotional ways that lead to direct action. Tax and investment policy may, in fact, define our life's options, but the connection is not always visible and direct to us. In this sense, the "invisible hand" of economics is all too apt a description. If our view of the economy is to change and the changes are to be institutionalized, we must find ways to ensure that citizens receive information on the economy and are equipped to understand and analyze it in order to make informed choices on the basis of *their* goals for a successful economy. To have economic illiterates is dangerous in a democracy because it means an inability to use concepts and analyze information, and it makes people susceptible to catchy slogans. Illiterates of any kind are easily fooled by the small print.

Spreading the Word

In Berkeley, every time we write a new budget or redraft our general plan, it is an opportunity to involve the public in building a shared base of information about our economic and social options. Similarly, I hope that the religious documents on the economy will be discussed by churches, synagogues—and civic organizations—across the United States. They need to be understood on both their levels of importance: (1) for the concrete programs they put forward, and (2) for their insistence on factoring ethical values into economic choice-making.

An interesting product of such a series of "teach-ins" would, I think, be a renewed appreciation of the similarities of the statements of different denominations. This will be very helpful in building solidarity because it will bring into high relief the shared ethical underpinnings that unite the world's great religions. As an elected person, I would hope to see a shared "ecumenical" economic vision emerge, toward the implementation of which individuals and organizations could work together on all levels of government—local, county, state, national and international.

The reference to the international level is crucial. The economic challenge of the emerging international economy cannot be solved within the borders of any particular nation state. We have become truly interconnected just as the great religions and poets have always insisted. The task of policymakers is to encourage consensus and build a set of institutional arrangements that will allow us to participate in a democratic and ethical way in the international and interconnected economy.

Religious institutions have an indispensable role to play by organizing their congregations, building an understanding of economic issues facing us, and encouraging analysis of the values and assumptions behind seemingly dry and technical policy choices. That will inevitably mean taking on entrenched economic actors from medical societies to major corporations. To refuse the challenge, however, would be to abandon the field to those who profit in the old ways from the old paradigm.

As one elected person, I can say with assurance that if members of the religious committee take on such an assignment, there will be many of us who will be at your side, and many more just behind you, cheering you on. The problem of those of us in public office who are sympathetic to these ideas is that so often we have no informed, supportive or concerned constituency cheering *us* on or challenging *us* to move forward faster. Indeed, the pressures usually come from the superabundance of those who represent old ways of thinking and seek to influence us through lobbying and campaign contributions. Unlike citizen volunteers, they do not burn out and go away; influencing us is very literally "their business."

That is one reason I so strongly support campaign finance reform that would include limited public funding at every level of government. It is absolutely necessary to put ordinary people back into the mainstream as sources of funding for political candidates they believe in—without this we cannot have the level playing field for people and ideas that is essential both for democracy and for serious consideration of the economics proposed by the religious documents.

We are all interconnected, and nowhere more so than in the policy arena. There is a role for everyone—the exposers of problems, the technical architects of solutions, the visionaries and teachers, the organizers and implementers. Taking religious documents seriously is an essential first step of the pastors' and rabbis' studies. I hope their proposals will not stay on the shelves but move out into communities and thence into the city council chambers, the state legislatures, and the halls of congress. If we have the energy, hope and will to build a movement around them, they have the potential to define our economic direction for the next century.

10. Organizing for Social Change

Karen M. Paget

Introduction

This chapter explores relationships between the church-based social and economic justice statements examined in this volume and possibilities for social action. As one who is unaffiliated with any denomination, I write from the perspective of having played many roles in our political system—from a locally elected official, a Carter administration political appointee, an organizer, and a funder of social change organizations in previous years, to an academic currently concerned with state-level public policy issues. These rotations in the different worlds of social action have left me fascinated with the intersections between them: What influences what? Who influences what? How important are ideas? Research? Electoral politics? Labor organizing? Local organizing? Individual empowerment?

It is not uncommon to hear that church-based social and economic justice statements are like research reports and other studies; however well-intentioned, they end up gathering dust on a shelf. Such cynicism, or dismissal, is often accompanied by despair: there is such a gap between the vision of justice contained in the statements, and daily manifestations of poverty and injustice, that one feels hopeless, and unable to act.

My initial reading of the documents in the above chapter left me with many positive reactions. A number of the statements are inspiring. By analyzing the economy—making it an appropriate object of ethical study—the churches are issuing an important reminder that economic arrangements are shaped by human, not divine, hands. Such leadership in demystifying the economy, and offering the possibility of judging economic transactions by religious principles, seems to me a necessary prelude to action. Nothing is more powerful than moral vision. The very fact that the churches have taken up the question of economic justice fosters and legitimates action, not only by church members but by the rest of us as well.

It took several readings for me to identify what bothered me about the tone and style of most of the statements as I thought about their implications for action and implementation strategies. Indeed, the single most striking aspect of the statements, considered from the point of view of achieving social justice goals, is *their relative silence on the question of transforming thought into action.*

When government is referred to, for example, the emphasis is on how much government there should be, rather than on how we can participate in government. The implicit view of "government" that emerges from the statements is as alien and abstract as most views of "the economy" usually are. Parishioners are mainly exhorted to "work for social justice" and to team up with others to achieve specific goals. There is surprisingly little reference to the most common form of collective action—voting—even though low voter turnout is one of the major problems facing American democracy.

At least three consequences of the omission are explored in this chapter:

(1) The emphasis on policies and programs in most of the statements is, ironically, not empowering: it tells people *what* to think and what positions to take, without teaching them *how* to think and act in accordance with religious and moral principles.

(2) There is little discussion of linkage between the citizen/parishioner and the political process, resulting in little guidance on how to participate.

(3) There are few references to empowerment strategies or collective action, despite the fact that many churches have played critical roles in social movements, and are still doing so.

Before discussing these three points in detail, I want to be clear about the strength of the statements. In raising the issues they do, the churches have taken up a central problem of democ-

racy: How do we judge right and wrong in a democracy? What is
the basis of moral authority in a secular political system? What
should be the relationship between an economic system and democratic principles? What is justice?

The statements are strongest, in my view, when they translate
religious precepts into criteria for judging specific proposals. The
Catholic bishops, in particular, set forth standards by which to
judge particular policies and programs. They say, for example,
that:

> The pastoral letter is not a blueprint for the American
> economy. It does not embrace any particular theory of
> how the economy works, nor does it attempt to resolve
> the disputes between different schools of economic
> thought.[1]

In their pastoral letter the bishops articulate six moral principles,
derived from scripture, emphasizing the dignity of the individual,
community, common good, participation, human rights, and special obligations to the poor. Most of the statements offer a similar
vision and method of judgment, whatever their differing views of
scriptural authority may be.

1. Overemphasis on Policies and Programs

Unfortunately, the force of the moral vision embodied in
most of the statements is blunted, surely unintentionally, by extensive delineations of particular policy options and programs.
While the various authors clearly intended to apply principles to
concrete situations and problems, many of the statements become
laundry lists of policies and programs, ranging from general
issues (such as housing, employment, day care, or social security), to even more specific policies (such as flex time, gun control, food stamps, and urban enterprise zones). One expects
something more far-reaching in the statements, a way of judging
proposals not only today and tomorrow but twenty years hence as
well. Such "position-taking" in the statements is, in fact, the basis
for most of the criticism in the popular press, and could be used

as a smokescreen to defeat the potential moral weight of these documents.

The most troublesome aspect of the statements' overemphasis on policies and programs is their pedagogy—the *way* they urge action and involvement. It is not the particular positions on these issues that is of concern; I might even agree with most of them. My objection is that the churches are doing my thinking for me. It is so often the case that attempted policy solutions turn out *not* to solve the problems they were intended to address, and disillusionment results. Attitudes, geared up for change, easily disintegrate into "see, we tried and failed." Response to the "war on poverty" is probably the best example of such a shift. The minority who have argued that the "war on poverty" was *not* a failure have found it increasingly hard to gain a hearing. A national effort had been announced, to lots of fanfare, creating huge expectations. But to have thought that poverty would be eradicated within a few years, or even a decade or two, now seems, at least in retrospect, foolish.

The Quaker social justice statements, however, convey a dramatically different approach from that of most other denominations in helping individual citizens understand social problems. Individuals are not seen as passive victims of the "forces of nature" or "the marketplace." Most of all, they are urged not to remain mere observers: "If we try to separate ourselves from it, we become simply part of the undertow of forces in the system."[2] Such a statement links the authority of individual experience with the moral authority of the church, by urging that citizens test received information with their own experience. Referring to this tendency in Quaker tradition, Kenneth Boulding is quoted as having argued, "Friends are also radical. Their authority is the light within, the present and personal experience by which past undoubted authority must be tested."[3]

This connection between the personal and political—or, to say it another way, the political made personal—was what was so powerful in the origins of the feminist movement. Women met in small groups, some informal, such as neighborhood coffee klatches, or in formal meetings organized by emerging women's groups, such as the National Organization for Women (NOW).

Their own experiences mattered; women's individual experiences were validated by being shared.

This concern to connect individuals with major issues is also a strength of the peace movement. When one sees a white cross on a well-tended lawn carrying the name of a Nicaraguan peasant on one bar and "killed by Contras" on the other bar, a powerful connection is made. Putting up the cross is a personal act that breaks down abstractions like "foreign policy" or "war." Such a gesture confronts in a non-confrontational way, simultaneously asking the observer to question his or her relationship as an American to the war in Nicaragua, and making a statement that for the particular householder the relationship is one of grief.

Some might argue that such gestures are symbolic acts of no real significance, especially in terms of bringing about an end to a war. To argue in this way seems to me to miss the point: once I am able to respond (the definition of "responsibility"), I become empowered. I become an active, rather than a passive, citizen. And, having taken that first, small step, the chances are high that I will take another . . . and another. Other people may follow suit, feeling emboldened by an individual act to act themselves.

2. The Matter of Political Participation

Most of the church statements exhort parishioners to political action—sometimes in dramatic tones—but say virtually nothing about how this is to be carried out. The Presbyterian statement, for example, declares that we must choose sides in the struggle between the haves and the have-nots, and asserts that "none of us can remain neutral."[4] Therefore, one must participate in politics, defined as:

> . . . an arena where competing visions of what is best for society can be debated and fashioned. By political activity we can protest what is unjust and work with others toward a better society, thereby responding to God's call to serve the cause of justice.[5]

There are few clues, however, as to the relationship between economic issues and what individuals should do. The Catholic bishops tell us that every citizen "has the responsibility to secure justice and human rights *through an organized social response,*" but they neither define nor elaborate what that might mean.[6] They refer briefly—in one sentence—to their *own* efforts through the Campaign for Human Development, which has supported community-based groups and empowerment strategies for the poor. They also defend the right of farmworkers to organize and belong to unions. They take an unrealistic view of the political conflict between growers and farmers, however, in urging farmers to act cooperatively, and saying that "farmers also must end their opposition to farmworker unionization efforts."[7]

The bishops' references to the role of government are determined by the "principle of subsidiarity," which means that "government should undertake only those initiatives which exceed the capacity of individuals or private groups acting independently."[8] Even these modest statements have engendered criticism from another denomination document that the bishops look too favorably on government as a solution to social problems.

When "government" is referred to in the church statements, it is generally the federal government that is meant. In one of the American Jewish Committee papers, the references are mainly to the executive branch of the administration; that congress plays an important role in decision-making as well is mentioned in an aside.[9] Only a few statements remind the reader not to forget the importance of state and local government. Government has little or nothing to do with you or me. It is distant and untouchable.

It is not just "government" that is distant from the reader. Frequently, so are "the poor," the reputed subjects of the statements. In most of the statements, citizens are urged to develop an empathy with the poor and to stand with them. Parishioners are urged to become advocates on their behalf. Yet a separation remains: it is still "them" and "us."

Note the contrast between that posture and the approach

articulated in several of the Jewish statements. Both the affluent and the poor have obligations: "Poverty is an affront to the dignity inherent in us as creatures of God. Consequently, those who can are obliged to help others avoid the degradation of poverty."[10] Poverty is not virtuous, but humiliating. In recognition that this humiliation lessened the dignity of the poor, the poor are encouraged to seek assistance from community funds and not beg door to door. More important is the rabbinical requirement to have the poor give something as well.

This principle, that even the poorest of the poor have something to give, underlies several federal programs: the Foster Grandparent Program, the Senior Companion Program, and VISTA—all administered under the ACTION agency. The Foster Grandparent Program, for example, assumes that low-income elderly have love and time to give to mentally and physically disabled young children. Similarly, senior companions are themselves low-income elderly who visit other elderly people, largely shut-in through illness, in their own homes. Each senior companion or foster grandparent is paid a stipend. The point is not that the stipend is sufficient recompense; it is not. Rather, the crucial point is that the entire program is structured to emphasize the dignity of the individual. These programs, unlike many administered by the Department of Health and Human Services, have never been attacked in the same way that other welfare programs have been. While the federal VISTA volunteer program has had a less sanguine existence, its goal also is participatory: to involve the poor in defining and working on community problems that affected their lives.

3. Empowerment Strategies

The churches' relative silence concerning empowerment strategies is interesting in light of their own history and involvement with previous social justice efforts, such as the civil rights movement. Primary examples are the southern black churches during the 1940s, 1950s and 1960s. Harry Boyte and Sara Evans, in *Free Spaces,* have developed the concept of free spaces, places offered by the churches where leadership could develop, education and study could take place, and information could be exchanged away from the dominant and controlling culture. They remind us that when Rosa Parks refused to give up her seat and go to the back of the bus, she was not just a weary worker who suddenly decided she'd had it with segregation. She had been part of a church-based movement, as were her parents, and had participated in alternative schools and study groups on segregation, such as that offered at the Highlander Folk School in Tennessee.[11] This does not diminish by one whit the courage of Rosa Parks; it simply acknowledges that such acts are the result of study, analysis, and organization. Parks was *empowered to act* by a network of people who were similarly courageous.

The Rosa Parks example in particular, and the civil rights movement in general, remind us of other key points as well. One is the commitment needed over long periods of time to work for justice; the other is a recognition that big changes start with individuals and small groups. One of the most difficult political topics to discuss today is the proliferation of activist groups in the United States since the 1960s. For example, Ray Dasmann's recent estimate of environmental groups alone ranged from a handful, before such landmark books as Rachel Carson's *Silent Spring* in 1962, to 12,000 or more currently.[12] There is no common nomenclature by which to describe what are alternatively referred to as "citizen groups," "public interest groups," "advocacy groups," "voluntary" or "non-profit" groups. One organization, The Independent Sector, which focuses mainly on voluntary and non-profit groups, has estimated there are nearly a million such groups in the United States—1.8 million if churches are included, 821,000 if excluded.[13] Public interest groups are local, regional, national, and even international in scope. Part of the confusion in discussing them in the aggregate is their sheer diversity.

While groups tackling economic questions are less numerous than, say, environmental groups, a recognition of their growth in the last two decades is important in thinking about implementing change. I would argue that their collective efforts over time, and their influence on the political process, are among the most salient realities of contemporary political life. This does not mean that economic problems are capable of being solved exclusively at the local level, or perhaps of being solved at all. I would argue, rather, that the lack of visibility and recognition of the role of these groups reinforces citizen passivity *and* an over-reliance on formal political processes, such as elections, for social change. As political parties weaken, collective-action strategies, through groups that mediate between individuals and the political process, become even more important. Of course, too much fragmentation by issue or constituency diminishes our sense of community and common ground. But the search for new common ground should not cause us to neglect participation in these modes of collective action that connect individuals with their larger political community.

In the nineteenth century, de Tocqueville wrote in awe of the voluntary spirit that informed this new country. People banded together in neighborhood and community associations to tackle—and conquer—otherwise insurmountable problems. More recently, the physicist Victor Weisskopf, who has worked for peace since his involvement in developing the atomic bomb during World War II, credited Physicians for Social Responsibility and other such groups with achieving what he and others had been unable to achieve over the last forty years. In making the link between aspects of one's occupation (making people healthy) and important political issues (nuclear annihilation), passivity is overcome. The U.S. physicians' organization is linked, in turn, with the International Physicians for the Prevention of Nuclear War, enabling individuals to engage in political action with the affiliates of other countries as well.

Conclusion

What are we to make of all this? First, we learn that *ideas matter*. When I returned to the United States in 1984 after observing the Nicaraguan elections, I wrote a lengthy description of that experience for my children because I wanted them to understand, more than anything else, the transforming power of ideas. Specifically, the role of liberation theology was the example I used—for regardless of the assessment of the doctrine's merit, there is no question that it has been a powerful factor in inspiring both religious and political revolutions. And nothing sparked more antagonism with then Archbishop Obando y Bravo than the role of the "popular church" and the "base communities" in Nicaragua.

Second, *the interrelationship between ideas and action* is reinforced. This is illustrated by a story from the torah as cited in Elliot N. Dorff's work for the American Jewish Committee:

> The question was raised: Is study greater, or action? Rabbi Tarfon said, "Action is greater." Akiba said, "Study is greater." Then they both said that study is greater because study leads to action.[14]

Studying powerful ideas, especially in concert with others, can be a significant incentive to action. In light of the statements under discussion, I would argue further that those ideas should include a demystification of the political process as well as the economy. Governing ourselves, or figuring out what to do next, should not be left to elected representatives whom we in turn petition and cajole.

One way to think about social change is to examine policies, programs, or institutions that we know about and that we think embody principles of economic justice. In analyzing particular examples, the chances are that we will find that ideas, leaders, ordinary people, or even the tenacity of one or two people made the program, institution, or policy a success. To think about change in this way helps to empower us as individuals. Individuals joined together with a sense of history, and guided by a moral vision of a just future, can engage in effective, sustained action even in the face of apparently overwhelming social forces.

Notes

1. National Conference of Catholic Bishops, *Economic Justice for All.* Washington, D.C.: United States Catholic Conference, 1986, p. ix.

2. Severyn T. Bruyn, *Quaker Testimonies and Economic Alternatives.* Wallingford, Pennsylvania: Pendle Hill, 1980, p. 4.

3. Quoted in *ibid.,* p. 31.

4. Presbyterian Church (USA), *Christian Faith and Economic Justice.* New York: Office of the General Assembly, 1984, p. 33.

5. *Ibid.,* p. 34.

6. U.S. Catholic Conference, op. cit., p. 60.

7. *Ibid.,* p. 120.

8. *Ibid.,* p. 62.

9. Gary Rubin, "Social Policy and the Poor," *The Poor Among Us.* New York: The American Jewish Committee [undated], p. 5.

10. Elliot N. Dorff, "Jewish Perspectives on the Poor," *The Poor Among Us.* New York: The American Jewish Committee [undated], p. 28.

11. Sara M. Evans and Harry C. Boyte, *Free Spaces.* New York: Harper and Row, 1986, pp. 48–61.

12. Comments by Ray Dasmann at a Future of California workshop, May 20, 1988, in San Juan Bautista, California.

13. Telephone conversation, Brian O'Connell's office, *Independent Sector,* May 16, 1988.

14. Dorf, *op. cit.,* p. 27.

11. What Do We Do Next?
A View from the Pew

J. Alfred Smith, Sr.

By this point we have studied numerous documents, read many analyses, reflected on a variety of responses. Where do we go with what we have learned? How do we run with all this information? It is not enough to have wisdom; wisdom is only valuable when it leads to action—action that produces change for the better. And those involved in initiating changes must include not only the people in power but the whole range of people in our society from top to bottom; not only church executives but church janitors; not only the formally educated but the people with self-acquired street smarts; not only the pastors and the rabbis but the lay people as well; not only those on parish boards but those in the pews.

We need to be specific. So in this chapter we will look first at how people in a black, urban parish church see the world around them, and then—more importantly—at how they are trying to change that world—how they respond, in other words, to the kinds of material this book contains. Members of other ethnic churches, of mainline churches, and of temples and synagogues should be able to adapt these insights to their own situations.

What We See

What do the folk see, who do not have degrees in economics or theology, who are not captains of industry or church leaders, but who are living on the very margins of survival? Two things at least:

1. *Everyone hurts.* Everyone is aware of living in a time of economic crisis. But few understand it or know how to cope with

it. Poor people feel helpless to cure the money disease that affects everyone adversely. Some feel that if they could just make a little more money their problems would be solved. Others fear (realistically) that their problems will *never* be solved, because the more money they make the more unmet wants and desires will be discovered, and the resultant increased spending will leave them further in debt than before. "Expenditure rises to meet income" seems to be a law of life.

On the political scene, the "successful" politician is the one who fights against increased taxation, while the politician who calls for increased taxes to fund social programs for the poor is unlikely to be elected. Special interest groups will simultaneously fight against tax increases while seeking to preserve the budgetary line items that will allow *their* group's programs to survive a tax cut, even though other groups' priorities have to be slashed. Churches have to allocate their resources in many directions, but pastors are slow to offend the tithers or large givers—one of the reasons why the most difficult sermon for most pastors is the "stewardship" sermon. Marriage counselors say that most marital troubles center on disagreements about how to use the money. Even the children in the home complain about not having adequate allowances. The problem of money (and lack of money) is an unwelcome guest in every household. Everyone hurts.

2. *Everyone wants to blame someone else.* While it is healthy to acknowledge how widespread the hurt is, it is not healthy to cast blame on others when we ourselves may be part of the problem.

Whenever there is a problem, however, our human response is to look for someone to blame—a response that is as old as the first couple in the garden of Eden. When God required an accounting from Adam, Adam blamed Eve who blamed the serpent who blamed God, and this game of "passing the buck" has been center stage ever since. Labor blames management and asks for higher wages and benefits. Management blames labor for rising costs or poor quality of production, and seeks cheaper labor by moving production to third world countries. People in third world countries, in their turn, charge that the invading multinational corporations rob them of their natural resources, rape their land, and leave their people poorer than ever.

Republicans blame the economic crisis on the Democrats for being the "big spenders" on social programs, while the Democrats blame the Republicans for creating the largest national debt in human history because of ballooning defense spending. The poor, already bearing an unjust amount of the national tax burden, blame the rich for not paying enough taxes. The rich blame the poor for adding to the tax burden by squandering the educational opportunities that would have fitted them to work on high-paying, skilled jobs, and accuse the underclass of cheating on welfare and being too "lazy" to work on low-paying jobs. The underclass blame undocumented aliens for stealing their jobs, and the undocumented aliens blame the poor for squeezing them out of the "equal opportunity" that the open arms of the Statue of Liberty seemed to be promising. Older people cry out, "The youth, who force us into early retirement, are to blame." Young people complain that not enough new jobs are available. Some white male workers accuse women and members of racial minorities of manipulating "affirmative action" programs to practice reverse discrimination.

So everyone has a simplistic reason for the economic crisis: it is the fault of someone else. There is not a single group that is willing to say, in the spirit of the Negro spiritual, "It's me, it's me, it's me, O Lord, standin' in the need of prayer."

Such convictions are self-sustaining, because what happens in society often forces the trapped poor to behave in ways that appear to justify society's ignoring of their cry for economic justice. It is an ancient game called "blaming the victim." Deprive a person of the chance for an education because of, say, skin color, and they say, "It's *your* fault you didn't learn calculus." Or fire a working father of six and then say, "How immoral of you to break into a grocery store and steal food!" The status quo tends to reward those who are suburban, industrial, "high tech," or male, which, from the perspective of the poor, often seems like rewarding the victimizer.

In the face of such injustices, those who propose a "putting people first" approach to economics are often called "danger-ous," or "bleeding hearts," or "idealistic romantics" whose im-practical ideas are a threat to the American free enterprise system that presumably has the blessing of God Almighty. People are conditioned to accept the status quo as the way things are *sup-posed* to be. No thought is given to the possibility that it might be "cost-effective" and highly practical for society at large to help the poor get training for skilled jobs, since otherwise they can do very little to save or invest their money to solve economic prob-lems. This is because *sheer survival is their number one prior-ity,* and survival is a basic human response that does not allow much time or energy to offer rational suggestions and solutions for the economic crisis. Can we really say that the poor are the only ones responsible for their plight? Let us at least refrain from placing the blame for the economic crisis on the prisoners of poverty, who, as every urban pastor knows, courageously make extraordinary sacrifices to survive degrading and dehumanizing conditions which rob their lives of dignity and value.

As we have already suggested, placing the blame is a negative response to the crisis, which hurts everyone. Therefore, all per-sons, irrespective of race, sex, religion, social class or national origin, need to confront the present economic crisis as an oppor-tunity to solve human problems with constructive actions in a new way. Only in this fashion can we act as persons who are concerned about making human life more human.

What Can We Do?

Let us look at a broad range of possible responses that could be made by people in the churches and synagogues.

1. *The need to be informed.* It is a new idea to many church people that studying economic problems is part of their job *as church people.* And many lay persons look askance at preachers, rabbis or priests who discuss economics from the pulpit when their professional credentials for doing so are notably lacking in almost every case. This makes it necessary to form study groups (perhaps using the kinds of material made available in this book) so that some of the rudimentary truths about the effect of eco-

nomic systems on day-to-day human life can be discovered. The recognition that people's paychecks, jobs, lack of jobs, size of salary, and so on, are at the center of such discussions soon removes them from the realm of the abstract.

Not only are documents available, such as those analyzed in this volume, but in most cases the different religious groups who have produced documents have also created study guides, cassettes, and videotapes to make such study come alive. (Lists of such resources are available from the Center for Ethics and Social Policy, 2400 Ridge Road, Berkeley, CA 94709.)

2. *The need to widen the circle of those involved.* Local councils of churches frequently hold conferences on ethics in economic life, and where that is not happening, congregations can request them to do so. The Northern California Ecumenical Council, for example, continues to sponsor learning events at Downs Memorial United Methodist Church in Oakland. In March 1988, the Council sponsored "Women Speak Out—Our Empowerment for Economic Justice." In May 1988, at the Sixth Congress of Peace and Justice Committees of the Diocese of Oakland, the Center for Ethics and Social Policy coordinated an investigation of theological foundations for a just economy, the federal budget, and health care policy.

In addition to such church-initiated programs, the legislatures of every state are mandated by law to sponsor hearings on the state budget, and on economic issues that relate to health, education, welfare, and the family. Lay people from every parish can be delegated with responsibility for participating in meetings of this nature.

3. *The need to dig in at the local level.* Each parish is unique. Therefore, since there are socio-economic, cultural and theological differences between them, no one parish will use exactly the same approach as others in addressing the issues of ethics in economics. However, there are four basic questions that are universal in all temples, churches and synagogues that seek to exercise ethical influence in the community. These are:

    a. *Who are we* as a congregation? Who are we in terms of our theology and our human makeup?

b. *Where are we* as a congregation? Where are we in terms of historic time and geographical place?
c. *What are we doing* as a congregation, and how well are we doing it?
d. *What should we be doing* as a congregation, and how are we going to do it?

The Allen Temple Baptist Church of Oakland, California is trying to confront the issue of ethics in economic life by addressing these questions. The parish is in the inner city—that section of the city which by virtue of age and adversity has undergone physical deterioration and is occupied by persons in the lower income level. The community around the church is inter-racial. It is a regional congregation whose members are persons of both the professional and working classes. Blacks, whites, Hispanics, and even some students from other countries comprise this predominately black congregation.

An active Public Ministries Committee works to educate the congregation by using the study-reflection-action method. Suppose, for example, it is necessary to confront the needs of children in the neighborhood or in society at large. Some hard facts have to be faced by such a committee if it is to function effectively. Here are some facts from which the committee must work in dealing with four and five year olds:

1. One in four children is non-white or Hispanic, among whom two in five are poor.
2. One in six has no health insurance.
3. One in five is at risk of becoming a teenage parent.
4. One in six lives in a family where neither parent has a job.
5. One in seven is at risk of dropping out of school.
6. One in two has a mother working outside the home, but only a minority receive child care.

Even more alarming are the statistics of what lies ahead for children just now being born. Of every one hundred children born today:

1. Thirteen will be born to a teenage mother whose earning power is necessarily low.
2. Fifteen will be born into a household where no parent is employed.
3. Fifteen will be born into a household with a parent earning a below-poverty wage.
4. Twenty-four will be on welfare at some point before adulthood.

For the Allen Temple Baptist Church, or any religious institution, to ignore such facts is not only to do ongoing harm to the children, but also to jeopardize the nation's future and to undermine the productivity of the national and world economy. The religious communities must, of necessity, cultivate a new generation of persons from a group of children who will *not* remain so disproportionately poor, under-educated and ill-equipped for life.

The philosophy of the Reagan administration to "let the private sector do it" has not produced any increase of private sector assistance in places like East Oakland. Tax reductions and business deregulation have not provided incentives for the business sector to increase investment and expand employment. In fact, several industries in the geographic area of the Allen Temple parish have moved to suburbia, and others have relocated in third world countries. The reduced rate of economic growth, the diminution of social programs, and the shift of the federal government from former support to passing the buck to state and local governments have all left East Oakland with a painful imbalance of programs and an awareness of how uneven the scales of justice really are.

In an attempt to work for change in economic policy, the Public Ministries Committee of Allen Temple also promotes forums on economic legislation. The Committee invites congressional and state assembly representatives to the church to answer questions about pending legislation, and to listen to the concerns of the people. Voter registration is conducted in the church courtyard after Sunday worship services. Members of the Public

Ministries Committee monitor the meetings of the City Council, the Alameda County Board of Supervisors, the Board of Education, and the Elmhurst District Council. These monitors keep the elected officials alert, and they provide the membership of Allen Temple with an adequate data base for making informed voting decisions. Frequent conferences are held on consumer education. Newly married couples are provided with economic counseling. A federally approved credit union provides assistance for members who are seeking low interest loans and an opportunity to build a share equity in The Allen Temple Credit Union. The credit union is also an excellent institution for teaching thrift and investments. All of this is desperately needed, since on the streets of East Oakland loan sharks charge fifty cents for every dollar loaned to people who do not qualify for loans from commercial lending institutions.

Housing and elderly care are two further sensitive and raw issues. Why should a woman in her sixties feel that she must use up her life savings, or even sell her home, to keep her mother in a nursing home for less than two years? Why should a couple married for thirty years be forced to get a divorce in order to protect the wife's income and assets, while the husband impoverishes himself to qualify for Medicaid-funded nursing home care? Why should a middle-aged woman be forced to leave her job to care for a severely disabled parent or in-law? The typical East Oakland resident cannot afford to pay the continuing inflationary costs of proper care for the elderly.

In an effort to reduce the size of this problem in East Oakland, The Allen Temple Development Corporation was established. This non-profit corporation now sponsors one hundred and twenty-six units of housing for the elderly and disabled. Plans are on the drawing board to build low-cost housing for middle and low income couples who desire home ownership. From 82nd Avenue to 105th Avenue, the decaying business strip needs revitalizing. With the assistance of private foundations, some seed money has been raised for conducting a feasibility study to determine how the business strip can be nursed back to new economic health.

Poverty caused by unemployment and underemployment is challenged by The Allen Temple Job Information Center, which is open four hours a day, Monday through Friday, each week. A Minority Business Directory is published every two years by the Business and Professional Men's Society of Allen Temple. Business ownership rates are lower among blacks than among most other ethnic groups. Most black businesses have traditionally been concentrated in small retail and professional service areas, where there are few employees and low gross receipts. Insurance is hard to purchase for black businesses located in non-white neighborhoods. "Redlining" practices mean that some of these businesses are denied loans because of their location. The Allen Temple Development Corporation is seeking to address all of these issues.

A Christian psychologist is helping the youth minister of Allen Temple in teaching courses in parenting and consumer education in the counseling of children and parents. A program in Teenage Pregnancy Prevention is sponsored by the Allen Temple Board of Deaconesses. The young adult women of the church sponsor a program that helps pregnant teenagers to give birth successfully and return to Oakland public schools in a special program that will allow them to work part-time and complete their education part-time.

Urban congregations need the political muscle and power of suburban congregations in attacking such further problems as plant closures. When a plant shuts down the local community suffers terrible economic and social costs. Both property and retail sales taxes drop, and for every job lost on the assembly line, three and a half other jobs are finally lost in the community. And the emotional, psychological and moral damage that results as a result of plant closures cannot be measured. Here, particularly, church coalitions need to be established.

Conclusion

No single congregation can do a great deal to relate ethics to economic life. But churches working together along with persons of other religious faiths and with all people of good will can accomplish much in making life more abundant, just and humane.

12. How To Use This Book: A Conversation with the Reader

Sydney Thomson Brown and
Robert McAfee Brown

One reader might finish this book and feel overwhelmed: "So much material . . ." Another might react, "Those aren't the issues I wanted to explore." A third might say, "Where do we go from here?"

The reactions are all legitimate and deserve response.

1. Yes, there is a lot of material. Religious folk are not known for succinctness when things they care about are under discussion. But the book has tried to sift through documents that in their original form are at least five times as long as the book itself, so some gain has already been registered.

2. If the issues raised are not the issues you wanted to explore, that may suggest an oversight on the part of the reporters, but it may also suggest that the issues you did not want to explore are important enough to others to be worth your exploration as well. How could that initial exploration of new terrain best be carried out?

The process will be short-circuited if attention is limited solely to the preceding pages, for the chapters repeatedly refer to, and often summarize, various documents by North American religious communities—Catholic, Protestant, and Jewish—and your discussion can be deepened by using at least some of the original texts. (The first Appendix outlines the contents of the documents and indicates where they may be ordered.)

The first task, obviously, is to study the materials critically, not only to discover their contents, but also to discover where you strongly agree or disagree. This is not a task for loners; there should be a group in order to guarantee a variety of reactions and a more lively debate. The group could begin with interested people in your own church or synagogue or labor union or community action group; it could include clergy or not, as you desire; and, ideally, it would involve people from a number of different religious and political backgrounds. (More will be said later about how such groups could organize.)

A few suggestions for making this initial exploration profitable:

(1) *Begin with your own situation* rather than with a theoretical discussion of, say, the meaning of "justice." What are the specific problems your community faces in relation to the economy? Are there enough jobs? Is unemployment on the rise? Who really holds power in your town? Who is hurting? Are you hurting? (Check Chapter 2 again to see what other issues you should be raising.)

(2) From this analysis of your own situation, *examine the various documents* (or, at least, for starters, the expositions in Chapters 3, 4 and 5), to see what the religious groups have said, or failed to say, about your concerns.

(3) Especially at the beginning, let the discussion be free-flowing, so that everybody's concerns and questions can be heard. Here are examples of issues that may be lurking below the surface:

Discuss: By what right do religious bodies speak about economic matters? (There is material in Chapter 1 that can help here.)

Discuss: How do the situations of the writers in this volume influence their appraisals of the documents? (Refer here to Chapters 6, 7 and 8, where the various "situations" include a corporation executive, a labor union leader, and two activists who are not white.) Further: How do the social and economic situations of the writers of the original documents influence *their* way of looking at things? Further: Does *your* situation influence your reading of the material? Such an exercise will raise a basic query: Is there such a thing as an "objective," bias-free point of view? If not, what kind of cautions does this raise for us in our study?

Discuss: In working for social change, what are the appropriate roles for the public and the private sectors? This is likely to be the most volatile question of all, since it raises the issue of relationship of government to social change. If some members of your group feel strongly that government should be given a significant role, be prepared for other members to call them "communists" or at least "socialists." The ensuing discussion will not be dull.

Discuss: What are the meanings of key terms that reappear in the various documents such as "a preferential option for the poor," "systemic evil," "structural sin," "empowerment of the powerless," "debt forgiveness," "economic colonialism," and so on? While many of the terms are new, the realities to which they point are not.

3. The original paragraph of this chapter concluded with a third query, "Where do we go from here?" The remaining paragraphs of the chapter will address that question.

A time will come when the study of the documents will begin to pall, and readers may think: "We can't just sit around talking; we've got to start working."

This is the point at which the group's real work begins. For the point of the documents, and of this book, is not to spawn a never-ending discussion group but to engage people in action for social change. (Chapters 9, 10 and 11 offer specific suggestions for initiating social change, from the perspectives of a political activist, a social planner, and the pastor of an inner-city black church.)

Beyond those suggestions, it may be helpful to provide a framework within which the venture might go forward. A possible framework for moving from talk to action has been provided by the five proposals of the Canadian Roman Catholic bishops, cited in Chapter 3 above. Our concluding pages will offer a brief elaboration of each of their five steps.

1. *"Being present with and listening to the experience of the poor, the marginalized, the oppressed in our society."*

It is not enough just to listen to just one group of people. It is important that any group be as diverse as possible: managers, secretaries, single working mothers and professionals, retirees, service workers, unemployed and working parents, white and non-white, rich and poor, theoreticians and activists. Academics, professionals, and middle-class citizens need particularly to hear directly from those who are hurting—women, people of color, the unemployed, the dispossessed. Actual stories, from real people, give reality to, and personalize, facts and statistics.

A few suggestions for procedure: Divide into groups of ten or less. Make a pact to listen to each other, and to hear each other out. Agree that you will share the time for talk in an equitable way, and appoint a timekeeper to give the agreement teeth. Remind yourselves that no one is "*the* expert" on life, that each person experiences the economy in a different way, and that each experience has validity. Above all, remember that your common search is for a fairer, more just economy.

Remember that it is not enough to "read about poverty," including charts or statistics, or to enlist a middle class member of the group to present the "viewpoint of the poor." All such exercises leave the non-poor isolated from the dire straits of the majority of the human family.

The experience that lies behind the creation of this book may be instructive. Over a number of years, various individuals and community action groups in the San Francisco Bay area began to discover one another as they worked from their different perspectives on such issues as plant closures, flight of capital overseas, sexism in the work place, rising unemployment, union-busting, and means of achieving minimal justice for the marginated. All kinds of viewpoints were present—Christian, Jewish, "secular," gay and lesbian, black, Filipino, Korean, Hispanic, white, middle class, and so on. Out of this diversity, amazingly similar agendas and working networks began to emerge. Working together toward a shared goal became the order of the day. So when it seemed appropriate to pull some of this thinking together in book form and provide help for others who wanted to relate religion to social order, a community of shared involvement already existed. By reaching out to a few more who would provide a still wider "mix," it was possible to assemble a group willing to share together in the creation of this volume.

The point is that the creation of such groups doesn't happen only in the third world. It happens in Oakland and Berkeley, and it is happening in many similar places in the United States.

As such groups are founded, it is essential to find ways (as the bishops put it) to "be present with" and to "listen to" the voices that some members of the group will not have heard before.

This will call for discipline among the verbally adept academics and theorists, a willingness to listen by those who are not used to doing so. But such persons may make an important discovery: those whom the bishops call "the poor, the marginalized, the oppressed in our society" have an intensity of feeling (growing out of countless destructive experiences) that often gives them a powerful eloquence. Going through such a process may take more time than listening to a snappy task-force report, but it can almost be guaranteed to produce better results.

2. *"Developing a critical analysis of the economic, political and social structures that cause human suffering."*

The step described above could almost be summarized as "telling one another our stories," sharing where we are coming from, describing what hurts, and beginning to suggest how we might respond.

After this period of building trust and understanding, however, some hard-headed analysis is needed. There will be different gifts among the members. Some will be gifted in social and political analysis; some can make connections with our biblical roots; some can articulate what it feels like to be tired, poor, overworked and underpaid; others can share what it feels like to be middle class, tired and pressed; still others can share what it is like to have no work at all and no place in the economy.

Start, therefore, by discovering the gifts of those present in the group. If more specific analytic help is needed, or a particular "voice" is absent, then search for help in the wider community. A psychologist could explain how people disguise their manipulation of other people. A sociologist or community organizer could show how groups—corporations, unions, legislatures, churches and synagogues—do the same thing. A political scientist could describe the parameters of the possible. A pastor or theologian could remind everyone of a vision of a new world that empowers people to a divine discontent when they fall short of it, distort its reality, or limit that reality to a few. New insights will emerge. Members of the group will become acquainted with "systemic evil" or "structural sin"—with the fact, for example, that few people are poor because they are lazy or untalented, and that most people are poor because it is to the advantage of our economic system to keep them poor in order to have on hand a large pool of unemployed people, available for hire to replace uppity workers who might ask for pay raises or help to organize a union.

3. *"Making judgments in the light of gospel principles and the social teaching of the church (and synagogue)."*

It is at this point that the heritage of Judaism and Christianity becomes so important. We need to look to those in our common heritage who have gone before and shared in our struggle—the Hebrew people, the prophets, Jesus, men and women throughout our religious history, a whole "cloud of witnesses" from whom we can learn. We do not need to reinvent the wheel every time we approach a new problem in economic justice.

We will not always agree with the teachings of the past; they have, after all, been used to provide justifications for everything from slavery and witch-burning to the glorification of the status quo. But as people challenge the teaching, there is always the possibility of self-correction in the uses made of the past. Nobody any longer tries to justify apartheid on biblical grounds, whatever other grounds they might still appeal to. That still leaves a long way to go, but it does suggest that growth and new insights are always possible. So we will not only test the tradition; we will also (which is more difficult) allow the tradition to test us.

It is at this point that we often stop. We "publish our findings," or we pass a resolution, and feel content. But the Canadian bishops take us two steps further into less frequently traveled territory.

4. *"Stimulating creative thought and action regarding alternative visions and models for social and economic development."*

Those of us in the religious communities tend to look for

ways to make our systems of political and economic life a little more just, or at least a little less unjust. We tinker around the edges or settle for halfway measures. This is certainly part of the job. Any small step toward justice is better than no step at all, particularly for those who have been the victims of injustice.

But the Canadian bishops tell us that that is not enough. If the boots of some in the society are on the necks of others in the society, it will not significantly help the victims if religious groups persuade the owners of the boots to relax the pressure ever so slightly. What the victims rightly demand is that the boots be totally removed from their necks so that they not only are helped in the healing of their wounds, but can stand tall themselves and deal with their counterparts on equal terms, having power themselves rather than being destroyed by someone else's power.

Such a scenario is not appealing to those who benefit from the power of the owners of the boots. Sharing power does not come easily to anyone, while grabbing power appears almost endemic to human nature. There is scant historical precedent of nations or groups relinquishing power voluntarily. And yet any "alternative visions and models for social and economic development" will by definition propose a realignment of power in the human family. No wonder the bishops are far ahead of the crowd on this one.

For some, however, this more radical option is real. They are involved in many "alternative visions and models" springing up here and there among the powerless. The best known, perhaps, are the Christian "base communities" in the third world, in which small groups meet regularly, usually around the subversive action known as "Bible study," to chart new ways of overcoming oppression and sharing a new life together. There are significant counterparts of these groups among many of the religious activists and community people in our own country as well. Small cooperatives have been organized in many places that exemplify different patterns of economic organization. New political organizations, dissatisfied with the choices offered by the mainline parties, begin to appear. Regional groups, looking toward the possibility of making their areas increasingly self-sufficient, are seeking to escape economic domination by large power interests more dedicated to profits than to people.

Further experimentation is needed everywhere, and it is one of the tasks of the religious communities to identify with and give support to such experiments, even as they continue the necessary day-by-day remedial "band-aid" assistance.

5. *"Acting in solidarity with popular groups in their struggles to transform economic, political and social structures."*

Simply thinking about alternatives, whether at home or abroad, is not enough. The acid test for all concerned people comes when they (read "we") are called upon to take sides, invited by the poor or challenged by the poor to enter the struggle. There should be no romanticism about this. "Acting in solidarity with popular groups" means taking on the power structures in our society that want no change, and probably want to move the clock back on a lot of change that has occurred already. The German theologian, Jurgen Moltmann, has described this as "becoming a traitor to one's own class," or at least being perceived as such. Whatever terms are used, to take this fifth step is to move from relative ease into the midst of "struggle," to make new alliances, to walk as companions with the dispossessed.

Not everyone will get this far, perhaps only a few. But those who do (and also those who don't) need to continue grappling with a heritage that clearly sees the plight of the poor as a top priority, and insists that the search for new methods of structuring our world, in conformity with the demands of God's justice, is the task of all, whatever their individual roles within that struggle.

APPENDICES

*prepared by
Ed Voris*

A Directory of the Documents with Summaries

1. United States Catholic Conference
2. Canadian Conference of Catholic Bishops
3. Unitarian Universalist Association
4. The American Jewish Committee
5. American Jewish Congress
6. National Jewish Community Relations Advisory Council
7. The Union of American Hebrew Congregations
8. National Council of Churches of Christ in the U.S.A.
9. The World Council of Churches
10. The American Baptist Churches
11. Society of Friends
12. Church of the Brethren
13. The Christian Church (Disciples of Christ)
14. The Episcopal Church in the U.S.A.
15. Evangelical Lutheran Church in America
16. The Presbyterian Church (USA)
17. United Church of Christ
18. United Church of Canada
19. The United Methodist Church

1. UNITED STATES CATHOLIC CONFERENCE

A. *Economic Justice for All, Pastoral Letter on Catholic Social Teaching and the U.S. Economy.* (1986) (188 P)

Contents

Chapter I: The Church and the Future of the U.S. Economy
Chapter II: The Christian Vision of Economic Life
Chapter III: Selected Economic Policy Issues
Chapter IV: A New American Experiment: Partnership for the Public Good
Chapter V: A Commitment to the Future

B. *This Land is Home to Me. A Pastoral Letter on Powerlessness in Appalachia,* 1973, (20 p.)
C. *Strangers and Guests: Toward Community in the Heartland,* 1980, (36 p.)

Available: U.S. Catholic Conference
              1312 Massachusetts Ave. NW
              Washington, D.C. 20005
              Phone: (800) 235 USCC

2. CANADIAN CONFERENCE OF CATHOLIC BISHOPS

Three documents have been issued recently by the Episcopal Commission for Social Affairs of the Canadian Conference of Catholic Bishops.

1. "Ethical Reflections on the Economic Crisis" (1983) (4 P)

   Introduction
   Economic Crisis
   Moral Crisis
   Present Strategies
   Alternative Approaches
   New Directions
   Guidelines for Study and Action

2. "Ethical Choices & Political Challenges: Ethical Reflections On the Future of Canada's Socio-Economic Order" (1983) (26 P)

Introduction	1
I—Perspective	3
II—Problem	8
III—Challenge	14
Resource List	21

3. "Ethical Choices & Political Challenges: Free Trade—At What Cost?" (1987) (29 P)

Invitation	7
1. Social Analysis (Observe)	11
2. Ethical Reflections (Judge)	16
3. Pastoral Strategies (Act)	21
Worksheets	25–27
Resource Materials	

Available: Publications Service
Canadian Conference of Catholic Bishops
90 Parent Ave.
Ottawa, Ontario K1N 7B1
(613) 236 9461

3. UNITARIAN UNIVERSALIST ASSOCIATION

No comprehensive statement on the economy has been issued at this time. However, 21 resolutions on this topic have been voted since 1961. A resource tool for social responsibility education and action is available which includes all resolutions adopted since 1961 related to social justice issues.

"Resolutions and Resources, a Social Responsibility Handbook" (updated 1988) (315 P)

The section on Human Rights includes a subsection on Economic Justice, pp 77–80B. This includes the following resolutions:

Poverty—1964
Economic Opportunity—1965
Freedom Budget & Poverty—1967
Poor People's Campaign—1968

Rights of the Poor—1971
Tax Reform—1976
Economic Justice—1981
"A Call to the Nation"—1983
Interfaith Action for Economic Justice—1985
Poverty & Unemployment—1985
Resolution Commending US Catholic Conference Economic Encyclical—1985
Ending Gender-Based Wage Discrimination—1987
Housing for the Homeless—1988

Additional resolutions related to economic justice are found in the Corporate Responsibility, Health, Hunger & Agriculture, and Peace & Disarmament listings.

Available: UUA Bookstore
               25 Commercial St.
               Manchester, NH 03101
               (603) 627 5818 $33.00

4. THE AMERICAN JEWISH COMMITTEE

The American Jewish Committee has issued a number of documents concerning Economic Justice issues. We include the following:

1. "The Poor Among Us, Jewish Tradition and Social Policy." Adopted 1986. (63 P)

2. "Spotlight on the Family, Public Policy and Private Responsibility." Adopted 1987. (56 P)

3. "The Newest Americans, Report of the American Jewish Committee's Task Force on the Acculturation of Immigrants to American Life." 1987. (30 P)

Available: The American Jewish Committee
              Institute of Human Relations
              165 East 56 Street
              New York, NY 10022-2746
              (212) 751 4000

5. AMERICAN JEWISH CONGRESS

No comprehensive statement on the economy has been issued at this time.

The documents listed below relate to economic justice.

1. Commission on Law & Social Action. Information Bulletin on the Jewish Rationale for Social Action. 1962. (4 P)

2. Federal Responsibility for Meeting Social Needs. 1982. (3 P)

3. The Reagan Budget and the Needy. 1983. (2 P)

4. Feminization of Poverty and Economic Justice for Women. 1984. (2 P)

5. Resolution on Hunger. 1984. (1 P)

6. The 1985 Reagan Budget and the Needy. 1984. (2 P)

7. The Homeless, the Poor and Government Responsibility. 1986. (2 P)

8. Gramm-Rudman and Revenue Enhancement. 1986. (1 P)

9. Testimony on the Minimum Wage Restoration Act. 1987. (6 P)

Available: American Jewish Congress
               15 East 84th St.
               New York, NY 10028
               (212) 879 4500

6. NATIONAL JEWISH COMMUNITY RELATIONS ADVISORY COUNCIL

NJCRAC is the instrument through which its constituency of 11 national and 114 community Jewish agencies jointly determine the issues of concern; what positions they should take on them; how they can most effectively carry out those positions; and which of the issues should be given priority attention in the coming year. This program is published annually as the "Joint Program Plan." We include the Economic Justice sections of the two most recent plans.

1. "Joint Program Plan" (1988/89) (60 P)

The section on Social and Economic Justice includes the following policy areas:

2. "Joint Program Plan" (1987/88) (71 P)

The section on Social and Economic Justice includes the following policy areas:

Available: National Jewish Community Relations
             Advisory Council
             443 Park Avenue South
             New York, NY 10016
             (212) 684 6950

7. THE UNION OF AMERICAN HEBREW CONGREGATIONS

No comprehensive statement on the economy has been issued at this time. The resolutions listed below relate to economic justice.

1. Unemployment. 1963. (2 P)

2. Equalizing the Operation of the Law. 1965. (1 P)

3. The Eradication and Amelioration of Poverty. 1965. (2 P)

4. Civil Rights and Economic Justice. 1968. (2 P)

5. Martin Luther King's Poor People's Campaign 1968. (1 P)

6. Welfare Reform and Income Maintenance. 1971. (2 P)

7. Social Progress. 1973. (1 P)

8. World Hunger. 1975. (2 P)

9. Economic Justice. 1976. (2 P)

10. Full Employment. 1977. (1 P)

11. The Budget and Social Welfare. 1981. (2 P)

12. Legal Services. 1981. (2 P)

13. Economic Justice for Women. 1983. (1 P)

14. The Elderly. 1983. (2 P)

15. The Homeless. 1983. (1 P)

16. Wage Discrimination. 1985. (2 P)

17. Health Care. 1987. (2 P)

Available: Union of American Hebrew Congregations
                  Religious Action Center
                  2027 Massachusetts Ave. NW
                  Washington, D.C. 20036
                  (202) 387 2800

8. NATIONAL COUNCIL OF THE CHURCHES OF CHRIST IN THE U.S.A.

The NCCC policy statements listed are the bases of a great number of more specific and timely resolutions:

1. "Christian Principles and Assumptions for Economic Life" Adopted by the General Board, September 1954. (4 P)

2. "Christian Concern about Unemployment" Adopted by the General Board, June 1958. (2 P)

3. "Christian Concern and Responsibility for Economic Life in a Rapidly Changing Technological Society." Adopted by the General Board, February 1966. (5 P)

Available: Division of Church and Society
National Council of Churches of Christ
in the U.S.A.
475 Riverside Drive Room 572
New York, NY 10115
(212) 870 2421

9. THE WORLD COUNCIL OF CHURCHES

1. *Gathered for Life* Official Report of VI Assembly, World Council of Churches. Vancouver, Can. 24 July–10 Aug 1983

2. *Statements of the World Council of Churches on Social Questions* Dept of Church and Society 1956 72 pp

3. *Ecumenism and a New World Order: The Failure of the 1970s and the Challenges of the 1980s* World Council of Churches. 1980 97 P

   INCLUDED

   "Adapt yourselves no longer. . . ." Biblical

Available: World Council of Churches
              475 Riverside Drive Room 1062
              New York, NY 10115 (212) 870 2533

10. THE AMERICAN BAPTIST CHURCHES

No comprehensive statement on the economy has been issued at this time. A number of resolutions on the economy have been issued:

1. Statement on the U.S. Economy. (March 85) (2 P)

2. Resolution on Tax Policy. (June 85) (3 P)

3. Resolution on Cutback in Employment of Minorities and Women. (June 85) (2 P)

4. Resolution on Plant Closings. (June 80) (2 P)

5. Resolution on Unemployment in the Eighties. (June 83) (5 P)

6. Resolution on Economic Justice. (March 86) (3 P)

7. Resolution on Welfare and Human Services. (Dec 80) (2 P)

8. Resolution on Fragmented Society. (March 81) (1 P)

9. Resolution on Labor. (March 81) (1 P)

10. Resolution on Migratory Labor. (Sept 81) (1 P)

11. Policy Statement on Agricultural Labor. (June 75) (1 P)

12. Resolution on Agricultural Labor. (June 75) (1 P)

13. Resolution on Family Farm Crisis. (June 87) (3 P)

14. Resolution on Food & Fuel Assistance. (March 87) (3 P)

15. Policy Statement on Human Rights. (Dec 76) (4 P)

16. Policy Statement on Military & Foreign Policy. (Dec 78) (2 P)

17. Resolution on Military Spending. (Dec 81) (3 P)

Available: Board of National Ministries
American Baptist Churches
P.O. Box 851
Valley Forge, PA 19482
(215) 768 2400

11. SOCIETY OF FRIENDS

There is no national agency or group that speaks for Friends as a whole. Friends are organized on a decentralized monthly meeting/church level, and "representative" statements are difficult to establish. The following are publications or policy statements by Friends' organizations or Pendle Hill which is maintained by members of the Society of Friends.

1. *Friends Committee on National Legislation*
   245 Second Street NE
   Washington, D.C. 20002 (202) 547 6000

The Jan 1982 Washington Newsletter carries the Statement of Legislative Policy approved on November 14, 1981. (8 P) This statement includes these sections:

I. "We seek a world free of war and the threat of war . . ."
   1. Building the foundations for trust.
   2. Developing international institutions.
   3. Increasing security by reducing armaments.
   4. Coping with current conflicts.
   5. Making needed social changes peacefully.
II. "We seek a society with equity and justice for all . . ."
   1. Governmental Institutions.
   2. Economic Life.
   3. The General Welfare.
III. "We seek a community where every person's potential may be fulfilled . . ."
   1. Civil rights and liberties.
   2. Special Trust Relations.
   3. Immigration and refugees.
   4. Personal and social standards.

IV. "We seek an Earth restored . . ."
    1. Stewardship of natural resources.
    2. Energy and nuclear policy.

2. *Pendle Hill Publications*
   Wallingford, PA 19086

   "Quaker Testimonies & Economic Alternatives"
   by Severyn T. Bruyn
   Pendle Hill Pamphlet 231 **$1.25**

Quaker Thought	5
Quaker Experiments	10
American Friends Service Committee	19
Community and the Economic Order	27
Basic Principles of a Nonviolent Economy	30

3. *American Friends Service Committee*
   1501 Cherry Street
   Philadelphia, PA 19102 (215) 241 7000

   No materials from the AFSC are included.

12. CHURCH OF THE BRETHREN

No comprehensive statement on the economy has been issued at this time. The following statements represent the most complete summary of Brethren policy on the economy.

1. "Christian Lifestyle" Adopted by the Annual Conference, 1980. (13 P)

2. "Christian Stewardship: Responsible Freedom" Adopted by the Annual Conference, 1985. (5 P)

3. "Justice and Nonviolence" Adopted by the Annual Conference, 1977. (11 P)

- Imperatives: Peace with Justice, Economic Justice, Human Rights and Liberation, Eco Justice   8

4. "The Church and Farm Issues" Adopted by the Annual Conference, 1974. (8 P)

    I. The Earth Is the Lord's
    II. Who Should Control Farming?
    III. The Case of Growers, Crew Leaders and Farm Workers
    IV. The Rise of Alternative Ways of Life

5. "The Farm Crisis" Adopted by General Board, 1985. (2 P)

6. "Resolution on Rural Community in Crisis" Adopted by the Annual Conference, 1985. (6 P)

Available: World Ministries Commission
                Church of the Brethren General Board
                1451 Dundee Avenue
                Elgin, IL 60120 (800) 323 8039

13. THE CHRISTIAN CHURCH
(DISCIPLES OF CHRIST)

No comprehensive statement on the economy has been issued at this time. The study paper and resolution below relate to economic justice.

1. "Economic Systems - Their Impact on the Third World" A Study Paper adopted by the 1987 General Assembly. (20 P)

2. "Resolution Concerning Priorities for the Christian Church (Disciples of Christ), 1982–85." Adopted by the General Assembly.

Available: Christian Church (Disciples of Christ)
Division of Homeland Ministries
222 S. Downey Avenue/P.O. Box 1986
Indianapolis, IN 46206 (317) 353 1491

14. THE EPISCOPAL CHURCH IN THE U.S.A.

1. "Economic Justice and the Christian Conscience" Commended to the Episcopal Church for study, reflection and response by the House of Bishops, 1987. (23 P)

The paper describes a paradox of prosperity and poverty.
- Insights of the Biblical Heritage
- Today's Prosperity—How Fragile Is It?
- Poverty—How Serious Is It?
  - Unemployment
  - Hunger
  - Poverty in Rural America
  - Healthcare
  - An "Underclass of Americans"
- Why Has Prosperity Produced Poverty?
- Role for Christians in the Crisis
  - Prophetic—Declaring Judgment
  - Pastoral—Building Community
    - Standing with the Poor
    - "Systemic" Causes
    - A New Theology of Work
    - Responsibility of Government
- The "Bottom Line" vs People
- Challenge to the Middle Class
- Signs of Renewal and Hope
- Limits of Friendly Persuasion

2. Economic Justice Resolution-C 030a (1988)
- Resolution (1 P)
- Rationale (3 P)

Available: Gloria Brown, Liaison
              Episcopal Church Center
              815 Second Avenue
              New York, NY 10017
              (212) 867 8400 ext 464

15. THE EVANGELICAL LUTHERAN CHURCH IN AMERICA

The Evangelical Lutheran Church in America is a recent merger of the Lutheran Church in America and the American Lutheran Church. There have been no new statements since that union, but pertinent documents have been received as "historical" while not official for the new body. The statements below are such.

1. "Economic Justice—Stewardship of Creation in Human Community" Adopted by Tenth Biennial Convention, Lutheran Church in America, 1980. (8 P)

2. "Community Economic Development as Mission." A Study Paper for Congregations and agencies of the American Lutheran Church. 1986. (4 P)

Available: Commission for Church & Society
Evangelical Lutheran Church in America
8765 W. Higgins Rd.
Chicago, IL 60631 (312) 380 2700

16. THE PRESBYTERIAN CHURCH (USA)

1. "Toward a Just, Caring and Dynamic Political Economy" Commended as a study paper by 1985 General Assembly. (37 P)

2. "Christian Faith and Economic Justice" Approved as a Study Guide by the General Assembly, 1984. (48 P)

3. "Elimination of Poverty and Unemployment" Report to the General Assembly, 1972. (5 P)

Available: Office of Community Development
           Presbyterian Church (U.S.A.)
           100 Witherspoon St., B-3704
           Louisville, KY 40202 (502) 569 5795

17. UNITED CHURCH OF CHRIST

"Christian Faith and Economic Life" A Study Paper Contributing to a Pronouncement for the 17th General Synod (1989). January 1987. (45 P)

Accompanying Study Guide (23 P)

Available: Hunger Action Office
                  United Church Board for World Ministries
                  475 Riverside Drive, 16th Floor
                  New York, NY 10115   (212) 870 2951

18. UNITED CHURCH OF CANADA

"The Church and the Economic Crisis" Authorized by the General Council, 1984. (12 P)

The United Church of Canada has issued two other statements on economic justice which are not included:

1. "Report of the Commission on Christianizing the Social Order" (1934) (14 P)
2. "Report of the Commission on Church, Nation, and World Order" (1944) (12 P)

Available: National Working Group on the Economy
              and Poverty
              Working Unit on Social Issues and Justice
              Division of Mission in Canada
              85 St. Clair Avenue East
              Toronto, Ontario, Canada M4T1M8
              (416) 925 5931

19. THE UNITED METHODIST CHURCH

No comprehensive statement on the economy has been issued at this time. The following represent the most comprehensive positions taken by the United Methodist Church on economic justice.

1. "Social Principles," a section of *The Book of Discipline of the United Methodist Church, 1988,* contains a statement on the Economic Community.

Property	103
Collective Bargaining	97
Work and Leisure	
Consumption	104
Poverty	98
Migrant Workers	
Gambling	105

The section on the Social Community, pp 97 ff, addresses the Rights of Women and the Rights of Persons with Handicapping Conditions (93).
The Section on World Community, pp 108 ff, deals with the question of transnational corporations.

2. The 1984 *Book of Resolutions of the United Methodist Church* contains numerous resolutions issued at the quadrennial General Conferences from 1976 to 1988.

Rev. Kim Jefferson of the General Board of Global Ministries has compiled a categorical outline of these as well as official church policy statements in an outline roughly correlated to the Catholic Bishops' Pastoral Letter on the Economy.

Available: George Ogle
              United Methodist Church
              General Board of Church and Society
              100 Maryland Avenue NE
              Washington, D. C. 20002-5664
              (202) 488 5600

USE OF THE INDEX

The Guide to References establishes abbreviations of the Source Materials listed in the Directory of Documents for use in the Topical Index and Biblical Citations below. The Guide identifies each document by title and source.

The Topical Index lists all documents dealing with a selected list of topics related to economic justice—identifying each by the abbreviation from the Guide to References, followed by a list of the pages on which the subject appears. Page locations are omitted for documents of brief length.

The Biblical Citation section of the Index identifies all passages cited in the documents—showing Book, chapter and verse, followed by a listing of each document citing with page location following the dash. Multiple citations are separated by a semicolon.

Topical Index of the Statements

Guide to References

Aged. See Elderly

Agriculture. CA :1 3, 106–120, 137–139, 180, 181.
          CA :3
          CC :2 11, 12
          CC :3 13
          NJ :2 56
          HC :8
          WC:2 53
          AB :10
          AB :11
          AB :12
          AB :13
          BR :4

EC :1   8
PR :1   20
UN   11
UM:1   99
Work. CA :1 49–51.
    :3   26
CC :1   1.
CC :2   5, 8.
NC :1   3
NC :3   3
WC:2   53
EC :1   14
LC :1   3, 6.

Biblical Citations

Gen   1–2   CA:3–13
         1:12   PR:2–7
         18   PR:2–7
         25   PR:2–7
         26–27   CC:3–17
         26–28   WC:1–84
         27   CA:1–115; LC:1–2; PR:2–7
         28   CA:1–17; LC:1–2
         28–31   UN–2
         31   PR:2–7; UC–11
         2:15   CA:1–17 CA:3–14
         3: 5   WC:1–84
         4:8–16   CA:1–18
         9   AB:2
         22–23   CA:1–18
         9: 6   AJ:1–27
         11:1–9   CA:1–18
         12:1–4   CA:1–18
         14:19–22   CA:1–17
         24:48   CA:1–22
         38:all   PR:2–4
         43:16–44:13   BR:1-1

	35–42	AB:2
	26:13	AJ:1–48
	27:30–32	BR:1–4
Num	26:54	AB:5
	33–35	CA:3–15
Deut	5:14–15	PR:2–4
	6: 4–5	CA:1–24; PR:2–3
	20–25	CA:1–19
	7: 6–8	AJ:1–29
	10:18	PR:2–8, 10
	18–19	PR:2–4
	19	UC–6
	14:27	UC–6
	15: 1–11	CA:1–20; AB:2; AB:5; UC–6
	4	JC:1–3; PR:2–31
	4–5	PR:2–4, 9
	7–11	UC–6
	8	AJ:1–40
	11	AJ:1–46; DC:1–329; PR:2–9
	12–18	UC–6
	16:19–20	BR:3–3; PR:2–10
	20	CA:1–21; CC:3–17; JC:1–3; PR:2–8
	24:10–11	AJ:1–27
	17–18	AJ:1–24
	19–22	AJ:1–33; UC–6
	21	EC:1–9
	21–22	AJ:1–24
	26: 5ff	DC:1–329
	5–11	CA:1–19
	12	AJ:1–23
	12–15	AJ:1–33
	30:19	AJ:1–43
	19–30	CA:2–11–13
Josh	23:all	PR:2–4
	24:all	PR:2–4
	24: 1–15	CA:1–19; BR:2–2

II Sm	12:all	PR:2–4
	12: 1–4	PR:2–5
I Kg	4:20–22	PR:2–5
	5:13	PR:2–5
	9:15	PR:2–5
	21:all	PR:2–4
II Kg	12:all	PR:2–5
I Chr	27:all	BR:1–1
	28:all	BR:1–1
Job	1:10	AJ:1–42
	38:4–39:40	CA:3–13
Ps	9:7–12	CC:3–17
	18	CC:3–17
	10:17–18	DC:1–329
	11: 7	CA:1–21
	12: 5–6	AB:2
	15: 5	DC:1–329
	23: 3	CA:1–22
	24: 1	CA:3–13; BR:4; PR:2–7; UC–11
	33: 5	CA:1–21
	34:all	DC:2–332
	35:10	DC:1–329
	37:11	DC:2–332
	37:25	AJ:1–31
	37:28	CA:1–21
	41: 1	AB:7
	41: 1–3	AB:2
	62:11	BR:3–5
	71: 1–4	PR:2–4
	72: 1–4	CA:2–10; AB:2
	72:12–14	CA:2–10; AB:2; EC:1–15
	85: 8	DC:2–332
	89: 6–12	CA:1–17

	18:11	PR:2-5
	24: 7	CA:1-19
	33:14-16	CC:3-17
	34:all	PR:2-4
	34: 8-14	CA:1-19
Ezk	37:10	WC:1-85
Dan	1: 8-16	BR:1-1
Hos	2:21	CA:1-20
	2:25	CA:1-19
	6: 6	JC:1-3; UC-6
Amos	2: 6	PR:2-5; UC-6
	2: 6-7a	AB:2
	2: 6-16	CC:3-19
	2: 7a	DC:1-329
	5: 4-13	CA:1-27
	5:10-12	AB:2
	5:11-12	UC-7
	5:20-23	UC-6
	5:21-24	BR:3-3
	5:22-24	JC:1-3
	5:24	UC96
	6: 4-6	PR:2-5
	8:all	AB:7
	8: 4-8	PR:2-5
	9: 7	JC:1-3
Micah	2: 2	CA:3-6; PR:2-5
	4: 3	JC:1-3
	6: 8	CA:1-vi, 21; JC:1-3; BR:3-1; LC:1-3; LC:2-1; UC-6
Zeph	3:12-13	CA:1-27
Zech	8:12	DC:2-332

	28:18–20	PR:2–6
	28:20	CA:1–24; WC:1–85
Mark	1:14–15	CA:1–25; DC:1–329
	9–14	CA:1–23
	2:17	CA:1–23
	3: 4	BR:3–4
	4:18–19	CC:3–18
	4:19	CC:2–5
	6:35–44	CA:3–33
	7: 9–13	CA:1–23
	8:34–35	CA:1–25
	9:35	UC–1
	10:21	PR:2–6
	10:42–45	CA:1–25
	12:14–17	AB:2
	15–18	UC–7
	28–34	CA:1–24
Luke	1:46–55	CC:3–18
	46–56	DC:1–329
	51–53	CA:1–26; WC:3–12
	52–53	CA:2–1
	2:14	DC:2–332
	3:4–6	CA:2–2
	4:16–19	CC:1–1
	16–20	BR:2–2
	16–21	AB:2
	18	CA:1–x, 26; CA:2–1; WC:3–12; BR:3–3; EC:1–2; LC:2–1; PR:2–6; UC–1, 6
	18–19	CA:1–20; CA:2–10; CA:3–16; CC:3–8, 18; DC:1–330; PR:1–7
	21	UC–6
	29	BR:3–3
	5:11	BR:1–4
	20–21	WC:3–12
	24–25	WC:3–12

	11–28	BR:1–2
	20:22–25	AB:2
	22:25–27	BR:2–3
John	2:13–25	CC:3–19
	3:16	PR:2–8
	8:45	CA:2–1
	10:10	UC–4, 38
	15:12	CA:1–33
	12–18	CA:1–25
	26–16:15	CA:2–1
	18:36	BR:3–4
	19:10–11	BR:3–5
	11	WC:1–85
Acts	2: 1–12	CA:1–25
	4:32	AJ:1–32
	32–34	CA:1–28
	32–35	CA:2–11; CC:3–18; BR:1–4
	43–47	BR:1–4
	44	CA:1–28; AJ:1–32
	44–45	DC:1–329; PR:2–5
	6: 1–3	AB:5
	10:all	BR:3–4
	16:14	CA:1–28
	18: 8	CA:1–28
Rom	1:25	CA:1–18; PR:2–7
	6: 4	CA:1–30
	8:1	PR:2–10
	18–25	CA:1–29
	19	BR:2–4
	21–23	CA:1–183
	12: 1–2	WC:3–3
	2	PR:2–30, 34
	14–21	BR:3–4
	13: 1–2	WC:1–85
	13: 1–7	AB:2

I Cor	1:26–28	CA:1–28
	4: 1–2	BR:1–2
	6:19–20	BR:2–3
	12: 4–7	UC–10
	12–27	CA:3–28
	16: 2	BR:1–4
II Cor	1: 5	BR:3–4
	5:17	CA:1–30
	8:all	AB:5; BR:1–4
	8:23ff	PR:2–5
	9:all	AB:5; BR:1–4
Gal	3:27–28	CA:3–29
	5:25–6:2	BR:2–3
	6: 2	AB:2
Eph	1: 9–19	WC:1–84
	2:13–14	DC:1–329
	14–17	DC:2–332
	3: 2	BR:1–2
	8	PR:2–7
	4: 1	PR:2–10
	2–3	BR:2–3
	32	BR:3–4
	6:12	UC–7
Phil	2: 6–8	CC:2–5
	6–11	CC:3–18
Col	1:15	UC–1
	19–22	DC:2–332
	2: 9–10	WC:1–84
	3: 5	CA:1–18
	9	PR:2–30
I Tim	4:12	BR:4
	5:18	CA:3–9
	6: 3–10	CC:3–18

I Pet	2: 9–10	CA:1–29
	4:10	BR:1–2
	4:19	PR:2–7

Jas	2: 1–7	WC:3–12
	5	CA:1–28
	5–7	CA:2–11
	6–7	CA:1–27
	14–17	AB:5
	3:18	DC:2–332
	4:13–5:6	WC:–12
	5: 1–6	CC:3–18

I Jn	1:8–10	CA:2–1
	2:15	PR:2–30
	3:10–12	CA:2–11
	15–19	CA:2–11
	16	BR:3–4
	3:16	BR:3–4
	17–18	BR:4
	18	LC:2–1
	4:19	PR:2–10

Rev	11:11	WC:1–85
	15	PR:2–4
	12:11	WC:1–84
	19: 1	BR:3–5
	21: 1–4	CA:1–29